Anyone can do magick!

What it takes is knowledge and practice. Color magick is the most effective, yet most simple method of knowledge and practice of all approaches to psychic and spiritual development. The knowledge can easily be gained through this book; the practice, which only you can provide, will start the process of developing your psychic abilities.

In this book you will find full instructions on how to meditate more effectively, and how to use color to stimulate the psychic centers or "chakras" that are like psychic muscles to be developed. Color meditation may also be used to unfold specific psychic abilities like ESP, clairvoyance, psychokinesis, etc. You will also learn to use color in divination, as in crystal gazing, numerology, the Tarot, and dice rolling, and you are offered basic forms of "getting the answers" to your questions with enhanced psychic abilities.

Also included are techniques of placket magick, the use of poppets (dolls), the making of talismans, sigils and magick squares, the use of treasure maps, and healing, all enhanced with color. You can also learn how to use color in your home and work environment, and in your clothing in relation to numerological analysis of any date and occasion.

Color magick is powerful, safe, creative and enjoyable!

About the Author

Raymond Buckland came to the United States from England in 1962. He has been actively involved in the study of the occult for thirty-five years, and an initiate of the Old Religion for nearly twenty-five. In the past fifteen years he has had twelve books published and has written numerous newspaper and magazine articles.

Considered an authority on witchcraft and the occult, Ray has served as technical advisor for the Orson Welles movie *Necromancy* and has also worked as an advisor for a stage production of *Macbeth* with William Friedkin (director of *The Exorcist*). He has lectured at universities across the country, and has been written about in many leading publications. Ray has appeared on numerous radio and tele-vision talk programs including *The Dick Cavett Show*, *Tomorrow* with Tom Snyder, *Not for Women Only* (with Barbara Walters) and the *Virginia Graham Show*. He is listed in a number of reference works, including *Contemporary Authors*, *Who's Who in America*, *Men of Achievement* and *International Authors and Writers' Who's Who*.

To Write to the Author

If you wish to contact the author or would like more information about this book, please write to the author in care of Llewellyn Worldwide, and we will forward you request. Both the author and publisher appreciate hearing from you and learning of your enjoy-ment of this book and how it has helped you. Llewellyn Worldwide cannot guarantee that every letter written to the author can be answered, but all will be forwarded. Please write to:

Ray Buckland
c/o Llewellyn Worldwide
P.O. Box 64383-047, St. Paul, MN 55164-0383, U.S.A.

Please enclose a self-addressed, stamped envelope for reply, or $1.00 to cover costs.
If outside the U.S.A., enclose international postal reply coupon.

Free Catalog from Llewellyn

For more than 90 years Llewellyn has brought its readers knowl-edge in the fields of metaphysics and human potential. Learn about the newest books in spiritual guidance, natural healing, astrology, occult philosophy and more. Enjoy book reviews, new age articles, a calendar of events, plus current advertised products and services. To get your free copy of *Llewellyn's New Worlds of Mind and Spirit*, send your name and address to:

Llewellyn's New Worlds of Mind and Spirit
P.O. Box 64383-047, St. Paul, MN 55164-0383, U.S.A.

About Llewellyn's Practical Magick Series

To some people, the idea that "Magick" is *practical* comes as a surprise.

It shouldn't. The entire basis for Magick is to exercise influence over one's environment. While Magick is also, and properly so, concerned with spiritual growth and psychological transformation, even the spiritual life must rest firmly on material foundations.

The material world and the psychic are intertwined, and it is this very fact that establishes the Magickal Link: that the psychic can as easily influence the material as vice versa.

Magick can, and should, be used in one's daily life for better living! Each of us has been given Mind and Body, and surely we are under Spiritual obligation to make full usage of these wonderful gifts. Mind and Body work together, and Magick is simply the extension of this interaction into dimensions beyond the limits normally conceived. That's why we commonly talk of the "supernormal" in connection with domain of Magick.

The Body is alive, and all Life is an expression of the Divine. There is God-power in the Body and in the Earth, just as there is in Mind and Spirit. With Love and Will, we use Mind to link these aspects of Divinity together to bring about change.

With Magick we increase the flow of Divinity in our lives and in the world around us. We add to the beauty of it all—for to work Magick we must work in harmony with the Laws of Nature and of the Psyche. *Magick is the flowering of the Human Potential.*

Practical Magick is concerned with the Craft of Living well and in harmony with Nature, and with the Magick of the Earth, in the things of the Earth, in the seasons and cycles and in the things we make with hand and Mind.

Also by Ray Buckland:

Buckland's Complete Book of Witchcraft
The Committee
Doors to Other Worlds
Practical Candleburning Rituals
Scottish Witchcraft
Secrets of Gypsy Dream Reading
Secrets of Gypsy Fortunetelling
Secrets of Gypsy Love Magick
Witchcraft from the Inside

Llewellyn New Worlds Kits:

Buckland's Complete Gypsy Fortuneteller
The Buckland Gypsy Fortunetelling Deck

Llewellyn's Practical Magick Series

PRACTICAL COLOR MAGICK

by

Raymond Buckland

1994
Llewellyn Publications
St. Paul, Minnesota 55164-0383, U.S.A.

FIRST EDITION, 1983
Tenth Printing, 1994

Cover painting by Lissanne Lake

Library of Congress Cataloging-in-Publication Data
Buckland, Raymond.
    Practical color magick.
    (Llewellyn's practical magick series)
    Bibliography: p.
    1. Magick. 2. Occult sciences. 3. Psychical research.
4. Meditation. 5. Color—Miscellanea. I. Title. II. Series.
BF1623.C6B75   1983   133.4'3   83-80173
ISBN 0-87542-047-8

Llewellyn Publications
A Division of Llewellyn Worldwide, Ltd.
P.O. 64383, St. Paul, MN 55164-0383

For Tara
who brought color
and magick
into my life

NEWTON'S EXPERIMENT
OF 1666

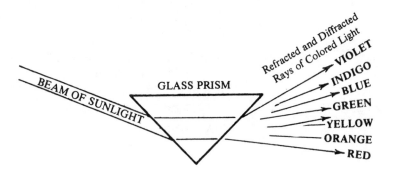

Contents

Table of Illustrations

INTRODUCTION

In the pink . . . Feeling blue . . . Green with envy . . . Red with anger. Purple passion . . . Rose-colored spectacles . . . A jaundiced view . . . the list goes on, showing color is very much a part of our lives. If we look closer at those opening phrases, we realize that color is also a part of our health. Since the beginning of time, colors have been endowed with *magick*. The ancient Egyptians used color in their Temples of Healing. The Chinese and the Chaldeans used it, as did the mystics of India, who associated colors with the *chakras*. Pythagoras used it for healing. You cannot live without color; it is your omnipresent companion throughout life.

But what *is* color? *How* can it be used?

Until the seventeenth century, it was believed color was created directly through refraction of sunlight. Sir Isaac Newton was the first man, in 1666, to break down sunlight into its component colors, as it were, using a prism and producing a spectrum. The prism diffracted the white light and divided it into seven bands of color: red, orange, yellow, green, blue, indigo, and violet. In actual fact, there is an enormous, if not infinite, number of perfectly distinct colors in light. These seven colors, however, are often referred to as the primary colors; other tints and shades being produced by mixing them. Here again, though, in the strictest sense there are really only *three* primaries: red, green and blue-violet. These cannot be resolved in any others.* These three colors, or *KINDS OF LIGHT*, when mixed together produce white. Further, the combination of any two gives the complementary color to the third, *e.g.*, red and light green produce yellow, which is complementary to the blue-violet.

Light travels at 186,000 miles per second. As it travels, it vibrates. Light is, in fact, radiant energy traveling in the form of waves. The rate of vibration can be measured in units known as Ångström units (Å), measuring one-ten-millionth of a millimeter. For example, the color red has a wavelength varying from 6200 to 6700Å. Orange from 5900 to 6200; yellow 5600 to 5900; green 5100 to 5600; blue 4700 to 5100; indigo 4500 to 4700; and violet 4000 to 4500.

Our bodies select, from the sunlight, whatever colors are needed for balance, the vibrations being absorbed into us. Animals and plants do the same. Our bodies themselves, of course, vibrate, for all things radiate energy. A chair, a table, a house, a flower, a bird; everything is vibration. This can be seen in the Aura and can be photographed through the Kirlian technique.

Science is still researching the exact way in which light

---

* They should not be confused with the three primary *pigments* familiar in painting and printing: red, yellow and blue.

penetrates the body. One school of thought holds that light is admitted through the eyes and thereby stimulates the pituitary gland, causing it to secrete certain hormones. It is a proven fact, however, that there is reaction from the body to light even without vision. It is possible the skin "senses" radiation through certain cells. My own feeling—which seems to be endorsed by the science of Radionics—is that when color rays strike the skin they produce complementary vibrations within the body which signal the brain and, whether by secretion of hormones from glands with resultant distribution in the blood or however, cause reaction of the body.

The principle of healing with color *(Chromotherapy* or *Chromopathy)* is to give the ailing body an extra dose of any color(s) lacking. The application can be done in a variety of ways, as we shall see. Basically, the red end of the spectrum stimulates, while the blue calms.

There are any number of experiments being conducted today, around the world, involving the use of color in such circumstances as work environment, living environment, education, nursing and so on. For example, the use of red, or even orange, in mental hospitals is asking for trouble. Blue, as a stimulant, has a cooling, soothing effect. Already, the stark white clothing of surgeons and their operating-room assistants has given way to pastel shades of blue and green (also soothing).

The study of color, for both therapeutic and magickal use, I term *CHROMOLOGY* (from the Greek *kroma,* color; *logos,* discourse). The actual use of color for therapy I term *CHROMOPATHY* (Gr. *kroma,* color; *pathos,* suffering). One of the joys of color, whether used for therapy work or magick, is its practicability. It is a tool which anyone can use, inexpensively, with little instruction and—perhaps more importantly — with no danger. As with Candleburning* there are no entities invoked in basic Color Magick. It is the use of a natural element in a practical way.

Color can be enormously helpful not only therapeutically and in the working of magick, but also in such areas as meditation, crystal- and mirror-gazing, tarot reading, absent healing, clairvoyance—in a myriad of ways embracing the full "spectrum" of the occult. We will explore some of these in the pages which follow.

Vide Practical Candleburning Rituals by Raymond Buckland, Llewellyn Publications (Practical Magick Series), St. Paul, MN, 1976.

COLOR IN MEDITATION

These days, when talk turns to meditation, there is always mention of TM—Transcendental Meditation. TM's results have been excellent, though those of many other forms of meditation have been equally so. But more and more, recently, I have been told by people in all forms of meditation, "I don't seem to be getting anything out of my meditation anymore." This is a comment from those who have been meditating for years and also is a reason for those who have now given up. Well, now the magick can be put back into meditation. Now you *can* get something out of it again; for now we can go a step further with *CM!* CM is Color Meditation, or Color Magick; and it transcends even TM, as many people have discovered.

Meditation itself opens the door to individual growth and spiritual advancement. It is probably the most effective method of advancement in all fields of psychic and spiritual development and, at the same time, the most simple. It can be done in a group or it can be done alone.

What exactly *is* meditation? The short answer is: it is listening—listening to your Inner Self, to your Higher Being, to the Collective Unconscious, the Creative Force, to the Gods Themselves. It can be all these things. And, through these things, it can bring you joy and peace, strength and understanding, life and enlightenment. It is a very ancient art, found throughout history and probably even pre-history. It is a quieting of the mind from the hubbub of everyday living, enabling you to get away, to separate yourself from your problems, your worries, hopes and fears. It can be a longed-for passive island in the midst of a sea of frenzied activity. That is not to say that meditation is not constructive. It is. In fact, it is far more constructive than passive.

The late, great psychic Edgar Cayce, in one of his readings (No. 281-13) said:"Meditation is emptying self of all that hinders from the creative forces rising along the natural channels of the physical man to be disseminated through those centers and sources that create the activities of the physical, the mental, the spiritual man; properly done (meditation) must make one *stronger* mentally, physically . . . And as we give out, so does the whole of man physically and mentally become depleted, yet entering into the silence, in meditation, with a clean hand, a clean body, a clean mind; we may receive that strength and power that fits each individual, each soul, for a greater activity in this material world."

Meditation and Kundalini

Meditation, in its present general form, has come to us from the East. Certainly, meditation has been practiced in the West for centuries but not to the extent found in the East. In Tantric Yoga, for example, meditation plays an essential

Figure 1

part in the preparation for such an ancient rite as *maithuna*. Today's almost universal acceptance and utilization of meditation has certainly been inspired more by the eastern teachings than by any other. Through meditation, your Psychic Force can be sent throughout your body to the vital centers known, in Yoga, as the *chakras*. This mysterious, very potent force, which dwells within all of us, is called the *kundalini* power.

Here's how it works. The spine consists of thirty-three vertebrae forming a long, hollow column housing and protecting the spinal cord. The cord itself extends from the fourth ventricle of the brain down to the coccygeal region. Through the center of the cord passes a fine conduit known as the *canalis centralis*. It is up through this central canal that the *kundalini* power travels when awakened. As it travels, it touches and vitalizes your special psychic centers, the *chakras*.

There are seven principle *chakras*. They are essentially of the etheric. Yet, they do coincide with various glands in the physical body: at the base of the spine in the perineum, midway between the anus and the genitals; at the fifth lumbar are the suprenal glands; at the solar plexus is the lyden; at the heart is the thymus; at the throat is the thyroid; at the crown of the head is the pituitary and, at the position of the third eye, is the pineal. These seven centers each have their own governing color. For the perineum, the color is red; for the suprarenal, orange; lyden, yellow; thymus, green; thyroid, blue; pineal, indigo and pituitary, violet. The seven centers correspond, as you see, to the seven colors of the light spectrum *(Fig. 1).* During meditation these seven essential centers are opened as the *kundalini* rises. It follows then, that the use of colored light, in combination with the meditation, will enhance this opening of the centers, reinforcing them and expanding and developing them beyond their previous limits.

It is through setting up the necessary vibrations that the "sleeping serpent" *(kundalini)* is aroused. These vibrations, then, play an important part in every one of us. To again quote Cayce (Reading No. 900-422): "All force is vibration, as all comes from one central vibration . . . Then we see the evolution of force in vibration brought up to the point wherein man becomes one *with* the Creative Energy, or the Godhead . . ."

This vibratory energy, and its relationship to color, has been measured. For example, it has been found that muscular tension, from the impacts on the retina of the eye, has increased under a green light from a normal 23 empirical units to 29 units. Under a yellow light, the tension has increased to 30 units. Under orange light, to 35 units and under red light, muscular tension has increased from that normal 23 to as much as 42 units. We can see, then, not only that color can affect you, but that the long-wave region of the (visible) spectrum—the "red end"—also stimulates. The calorific rays of red, in fact, can raise your temperature, increase your circulation, and quicken your heart-beat. The short-wave region—the "blue end"—has the reverse influence. This is the basis for the use of color in healing.

How to Meditate

But, let us return to meditation. Most people meditate in a wide variety of places, wearing ordinary, everyday clothing. This is fine and can certainly be useful. For example, if the only time you can meditate is when traveling to work on the subway, do it. But to get more out of meditation *you must put more into it.* First of all, meditate at the same time every day. Whether it be morning, afternoon, or evening is up to you. There are different types of people: some of us are "night people", others of us are "day people". Meditate at the time of day which *feels* best to you. If in doubt, here is a guide: find out (if you don't already know) what time of day, or night, you were born. Meditate at the time most conveniently close to your birth time as you can. You may find this is the "right" time for you.

Meditate somewhere where you will not be disturbed and where it is as quiet as possible—the back of the house, away from traffic noise, perhaps. The actual physical position you adopt for meditation can again be to suit yourself. You may sit in the yoga position, you may prefer to sit on your heels, or sit in a chair, or lay flat on your back. The important thing, however, is to *have your spine straight.* I personally recommend that you sit in a comfortable straight-backed chair, one in which you can sit well back—with your spine straight—yet still have your feet flat on the floor. The chair should preferably have arms to it, on which you can rest your arms. It need not have a high back, in fact it is better if it does not.

The CM Robe

Recommended is loose clothing. Particularly recommended is *THE C M ROBE.*

We have discussed the association of colors with the *chakras* and the desirability of stimulating those colors/*chakras*. This can be accomplished beautifully by the simple wearing of a robe designed specifically for Color Meditation. Any refinement of shape can be made to suit your individual whim—but remember to not make it tight-fitting. The material should be pure white. In addition to the robe itself you whould have a head-covering, also white and loose-fitting. This hat should have a front (point) which comes down to cover the space between the eyes, where the "third eye" is located.

Up the front of the robe cut out large circles (approximately six inches in diameter, suggested) at the areas coinciding with the *chakra* positions. Now fill in these holes with circles of colored material (same type material as the robe. I would suggest using silk throughout though other material, such as linen, would do as well), the colors corresponding to the *chakra* colors/positions: red for the perineum; orange for the suprarenal; yellow the lyden; green the thymus; blue the thyroid; indigo the pineal (on the hat point); and violet the pituitary or crown *(Fig. 2a)*. Do *not* simply sew the colored circles on to the uncut robe. Cut out the white circle first, in this way the color goes right through. You can also then use the cut white circle as a pattern for the colored one. An alternative to the circles, which you may prefer, is to use whole bands of color going right around the

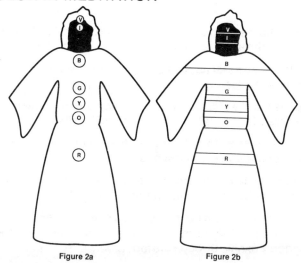

Figure 2a   Figure 2b

the robe *(Fig. 2b).* Do not use any other colored decoration on the robe.

When wearing the CM Robe for meditation wear nothing beneath it. In this way, interference is eliminated between the colors and the body. If it is possible, do your meditation before a window (preferably open). If not, then let a white electric light—incandescent rather than fluorescent—be shining on you. Some people prefer to do their meditation in darkness or near-darkness. If this is your preference then still follow these instructions, using the white light, as a *preliminary.* I will later indicate how to proceed from there.

Sit comfortably, relaxing the body as much as possible without slumping or allowing the spine to curve. Help loosen tight muscles by doing the following exercises:

- Allow the head to fall forward on the chest. Breathe deeply in and out three times. Return to the upright position.

- Allow the head to tip fully backwards. Breathe deeply in and out three times. Return to the upright position.

- Tip the head as far as possible to the left. Breathe in and out three times. Return to the upright position.

- Tip the head as far as possible to the right. Breathe in and out three times. Return to the upright position.

- Allow the head to fall forward, then move it in a circle, counterclockwise, three times.

- Repeat the last exercise, moving the head clockwise three times. Return to the upright position.

- Breathe in, through the nose, with a number of short, sharp intakes until the lungs are full. Hold it a moment, then suddenly exhale through the mouth with a "Hah" sound. Do this three times.

- Breathe in slowly and fully, through the right nostril (hold the left one closed, if necessary), feeling the stomach balloon out as you do so. Hold it a moment, then exhale slowly through the mouth, flattening the stomach as you do so. This exercise moves all the stale air from the bottom of the lungs. Do this three times.

- Repeat the last exercise, breathing in this time through the left nostril, and out through the right nostril. Do this three times.

Now, with your body relaxing and breathing normally but deeply, concentrate your thoughts until you can imagine your whole body encased in a globe of white light. Feel the luminous energy charging your whole body. After a few moments of this, see the light gradually turning to red. As it becomes red, see it form into a cone shape, the tip of which is directed at your perineum *chakra*. As you continue to breathe deeply, see and feel the red light slowly flow into the

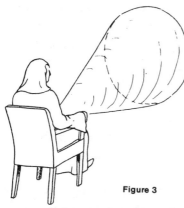

Figure 3

perineum area. When you feel you have absorbed all that you can, see the all-encompassing globe of white light return.

Next, let the white light give way to a cone of orange. The point of this cone is directed at the suprarenal *(Fig. 3).* Again, as you breathe deeply, feel the orange light pouring down the cone and into your body.

Continue in this fashion, working through all the *chakras* and drawing all their respective colors into you. Finish with the all-encompassing white light which you had at the start. If you find it difficult to envision the different colors, set up a chart where you can see them before you. A good one can be made from rectangles of colored construction paper— the sort used in schools, obtainable from any stationery store— pasted on a larger black sheet *(Fig. 4).* A glance at the chart each time sets the required color in your mind.

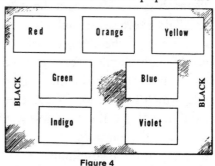

Figure 4

Having completed these preliminaries you will now enter an incredibly deep and satisfying meditation. One of the first rewards, will be tremendous peace of mind and inner satisfaction. If you prefer to meditate in reduced light, draw the blind over the window or extinguish the white light and settle back. At the end of the meditation period, before returning to "normalcy", imagine yourself for a few minutes encompassed in the globe of white light.

Group Meditation

Group meditation can bring enormous satisfaction. The interaction of each person's vibrations work in a complementary manner resulting in tremendous psychic achievement. When meditating alone you may, once in a while, experience an "off" day. This is never the case with group meditation. In fact, for this reason, many people will only meditate with a group.

In group meditation, I again recommend the wearing of the C M Robe. In all meditative situations—and, as we shall see, in most other areas of occult practice—the C M Robe serves as a remarkable catalyst. The group should seat themselves in a circle and should go through their breathing and light exercises in their own time. At the completion, by everyone, of the *chakra* color-reinforcement, the white electric light should be extinguished, or blinds drawn, and the circle should then be illuminated by a *blue* light. In the group with which I work, we use a Westinghouse 100-watt "color tone" floodlight. It is available just about everywhere and is ideal for the purpose. This blue light should remain on throughout the meditation.

If you already meditate and hesitate to encompass Color Magick in what may have become your set procedure, try this simple test. Do your meditation just as you normally would—but *do it in the light of a blue bulb.* That's all. I guarantee you will have one of the best meditations you have ever had!

Some final words on meditation generally. You must meditate consistently. Some say twice a day: morning and evening, for twenty minutes each period. I personally think once a day for fifteen minutes is sufficient. But, whatever you choose, be consistent. Do it the same time(s) *each* day and *every* day. Don't just do it occasionally, as the fancy strikes you.

When you first start to meditate you will find it difficult to sit still for more than a few minutes at a time. Your body will want to fidget; you will perhaps feel a great itch developing, demanding to be scratched! It takes a little time, but you will soon become master of your physical self. Ignore the itch, however much it screams. It will go away.

Meditation should not be confused with prayer. When you pray you petition deity. You are asking. In meditation you are *listening;* perhaps you will hear the answers to your prayers. Prayer and meditation complement one another.

People who have never meditated before have said to me: "But how do you keep your mind completely blank for a quarter of an hour?" The answer is: "you don't!" It would be, I think, an impossibility. No, what you do is focus your mind on a concept. In TM one is given a *mantra* on which to focus. A *mantra* is a word/sound of spiritual, frequently religious, significance which serves as a focal point for the mind while allowing the psychic centers to open up and receive what may be forthcoming. In the meditation taught by Edgar Cayce, you focus on an affirmation; a short phrase which capsulates thoughts relevant to approaches in a search for God/ess.

Neither *mantras* nor affirmations are necessary. You can dwell on any word(s) or on a symbol. If you are seeking answers to questions, then concentrate on those questions. Try to break them down to their lowest denominators, to the fewest words possible. Study those words and see them, as it were, in your mind, in the position of the third eye. Place them there, at the pineal gland, and let your mind dwell on them. Gradually answers will come. Perhaps not immediately, but they will come. Often, when you reach this stage, you are suddenly aware of a white light. It is both within us and about us. This does not always happen, but when it does, it is one of the most satisfying of occult experiences.

2

COLOR IN PSYCHIC DEVELOPMENT

There are many people who seem, very obviously, to have ESP. The sort of people who know that the telephone is going to ring before it actually does; who know who is on the other end of the line before they pick up the receiver. These people have their psychic power developed quite naturally. Often times other people envy them, thinking "I could never be like that. I don't have any such powers." Yet that is not true. *Everyone* has that power. *Everyone* has psychic ability. It is just that in some, as we have seen, the power comes out naturally, while in others it has to be drawn out.

There are many different ways to draw out your psychic power. In this chapter I will show a few of the ways, utilizing color for psychic development. I will deal with ESP (Extra Sensory Perception); clairvoyance (literally, "clear seeing"); clairaudience (clear hearing); clairsentience (clear sensing); psychokinesis (moving objects without physical contact); and other allied practices.

First Exercise
Take seven pieces of colored material, each in one of the

13

seven primary colors. The pieces should all be the same size and of the same material. I use squares of colored felt. You can use whatever you like (cloth, silk, felt, construction paper, cardboard) so long as all are the same in size and material. Now, sit quietly and go through the breathing exercises detailed in Chapter One *(Meditation)*. Correct breathing is a very important part of psychic development and these exercises should *always* be performed before *any* experiment.

Sitting at a table, close your eyes and mix up the colors in front of you. Then take one color and, with your eyes kept closed, hold it between your hands, palm to palm. Concentrate on the material and see if you can sense (*not* "guess") the color you hold. Does it feel warm, or cool? Do your palms or fingers tingle? Hold it to your forehead and to your cheek. Any different reaction? When you feel you know the color, open your eyes and check. If you are wrong don't worry. Make a note of your choice. Take a sheet of paper and draw three columns *(Fig. 5)*: column one should be headed "COLOR". In that write the actual color you find yourself holding. Column two is headed "SENSE". In that write the color that you *thought* you held. Column three is "SENSA-TIONS", and there you should write any reactions you

COLOR	SENSE	SENSATIONS
Red	Red	Warnth, Love
Green	Violet	Pleasant, Cool
Yellow		
Blue	Green	Cool, Trees
Red	Orange	Heat, Danger
Indigo		

Figure 5

have. For example, you might have felt the color was cool and vaguely unpleasant. Or it might have felt warm and friendly. Write down anything you felt even if, on the face of it, it doesn't seem necessarily applicable to a color.

Put the color back with the rest and again close your eyes and mix them up. Go through the same procedure: mix the colors, pick up one, hold it and try to sense it, note the results.

Keep this up for at least ten minutes, then sit back and check your results. They should prove interesting. Don't be disappointed if most of your choices were wrong. A "close" is almost as good as a "correct" (e.g. if the color was red and you thought it was orange). Examine the sensations. The red end of the color scale is the hot end; the blue is the cold. Red will stimulate while blue will calm.

Let's take time here to have a look at the results of a test that was conducted with children in a school in England. The children were shown fabrics of different colors and asked to write down their feelings about these colors. This was the result:

RED: Danger. Anger. Fire. Love. Thirst. Mean. Hate.
ORANGE: Woods, Autumn. Warm. Kind. Fire.
YELLOW: Summer. Sleep. Glad. Light. Easter. Sick.
GREEN: Cool. Nice. Flowers. Ocean. Picnic. Reading. Snakes.
BLUE: Water. Cool. Lazy. Home. Frost. Lonely.
INDIGO: Soft. Gentle. Sweet. Prayers.
VIOLET: Sad. Church. Love. Warmth.

I will not attempt to analyze these, but from this list you may find certain parallels with your own. It is interesting, I think, that there are one or two seeming contradictions contained in the list. For example, Red stimulates both Love and Hate; Yellow both Gladness and Sickness.

Traditional Associations

In the metaphysical world colors do, traditionally, have certain associations (for example, those utilized in Candle-burning Magick). The traditional associations are as follows:

COLOR CHART

RED	Strength, Health, Vigor, Sexual Love, Danger, Charity
ORANGE	Encouragement, Adaptability, Stimulation, Attraction, Plenty, Kindness
YELLOW	Persuasion, Charm, Confidence, Jealousy, Joy, Comfort
GREEN	Finance, Fertility, Luck, Energy, Charity, Growth
BLUE	Tranquility, Understanding, Patience, Health, Truth, Devotion, Sincerity
INDIGO	Changeability, Impulsiveness, Depression, Ambition, Dignity
VIOLET	Tension, Power, Sadness, Piety, Sentimentality

It is useful to know these associations for purposes of psychic development. This will be explained more fully as I go.

Second Exercise

The transitional period between waking and sleeping is known as the *hypnogogic state;* between sleeping and waking is the *hypnopompic state.* Either of these times is excellent for psychic experimentation.

Try this experiment/exercise. Take seven colored pieces

of material (the seven primary colors) and place each in a separate window-envelope. Seal the envelopes. With the windows downwards, mix them up. Just before you go to bed pick one envelope at random, and place it under your pillow, taking care that you don't see the color through the envelope window. Just as you are on the point of falling asleep, concentrate your thoughts on the envelope under the pillow, trying to pick up the color inside. There is a very simple way to do this. Lie on your back and, with your arms at your sides, raise one hand and fore-arm (bent at the elbow) straight up in the air. As you fall into sleep your hand and arm will fall back across you, waking you again. *At that moment* try to sense the color beneath your pillow. Write it down (however roughly, and quickly!) then go to sleep.

As soon as you wake in the morning again write down the color you *then* sense, along with any sensations, thoughts, feelings associated with it. The color you sense as you wake (in the hypnopompic state) may well be different from that you sensed in the hypnogogic state. Don't worry. List them both. You will need three headings on your recording sheet: COLOR (as seen through the envelope's window in the morning); HYPNOGOGIC (falling asleep sensation); HYPNOPOMPIC (awakening sensation).

Put the envelope back with the others and mix them. Repeat the experiment the next night, and for a total of twenty-one nights. From this, as well as seeing how well you are able to pick-up the colors, generally, you will see which is the better time for you to do your psychic work: evening or morning.

Third Exercise

A very simple, yet effective, ESP test can be done using twelve playing-cards. From a deck of regular playing-cards take out the eight, nine, ten of clubs; eight, nine, ten of spades; eight, nine, ten of hearts; and the eight, nine, ten of diamonds (these are the twelve cards bearing the largest number of "pips"—most useful for differentiating between red and black, which you are going to do). Shuffle these twelve cards and then lay them, face down, in a row on the table in front of you.

Now, going from left to right, try to sense each card as to whether it is red or black. That's all. Don't concern yourself with the actual suit, or the value; just whether it is red or black.

You may find it a help to gently lay your fingertips on the back of each card, or, perhaps, to hold the palm of the the hand over it. Experiment. Write down your guesses (senses). Then turn the cards over and see how correct you were.

Shuffle the cards and repeat the experiment. Always work from left to right. Do it ten times, at least, keeping score of your results.

Since there are only two possible answers to each guess expect an *average* of six correct each run, for chance. If chance alone is at work, therefore, you will have approximately sixty correct in going through ten times. If, however, you find you have considerably more than sixty correct (*or* considerably less) then ESP is at work. For example, if you have seventy-three correct, the odds are twenty to one against chance; seventy-eight correct and the odds are one hundred to one against chance. Of course, the more times you go through, the more accurate a picture you will get. Here are the odds for various runs through:

NUMBER OF RUNS	CHANCE SCORE	GOOD (20:1 against chance)	EXCELLENT (100:1 against chance)
10	60	73	78
20	120	144	152
30	180	215	222
40	240	286	295
50	300	356	365

If you want to make the above experiment more interesting, and more of a challenge, then use photographs of people instead of playing-cards: six colored photographs and six black-and-white. You will probably have to put each photograph in an envelope so that they all appear the same. Try to simply differentiate between the colored and the black-and-white. It will be more difficult because, from the pictures, you will also be getting feelings, emotions, health, etc., etc., which could be confusing. It might help a little to have the colored photographs all of women and the black-and-white all of men.

Fourth Exercise

Imagery is a step towards clairvoyance. Sit in a comfortable straight-backed chair. The one you use for meditation is ideal. Wear your C M Robe for this experiment. Close your eyes and do your breathing exercises. Then, after a moment's quiet, imagine that there is a large tube standing on the floor in front of you. It is like those large cardboard tubes used for mailing posters, etc. See it standing, on end, in front of you. In your mind, reach out and take the tube. Lift it up and look through it, as a child might in pretending it is a telescope. This is your psychic telescope to other worlds, other realities.

See the tube stretching away in front of you. It is large enough that you can look down it with both eyes (keep your actual eyes closed, of course). See it, in your mind's eye, stretching away off into the distance. There is no weight to it so it can stretch away for miles, if necessary. At the far end of the tube see the color green.

Now, much like with an actual telescope or the zoom-lens of a movie camera, bring your tube into focus. Shorten it. Let the far end move in towards you and see that the green is now the green of grass. See a vast field of grass, perhaps with green trees off to one side. Shorten the tube again. Bring that scene in closer and closer till you can see all the details. If you want to you can focus on just one small item, just one blade of grass.

Now extend the tube again and let the end be the general green color. Change the green to blue. At the far end of your tube is the color blue. Gradually bring it into focus, shortening the tube. See now that the blue is a large armchair. It is in a room. See the room, and all its details. You can move the end of the tube around as you wish, getting either a general view of the whole room or closing in on a single piece of furniture or item of decoration.

In clairvoyance you can see such a room as the room of the person you wish to contact. As you look at it you can make the door open and bring whomever you wish into the room. Another way to contact a person is to go through the above procedure but, in moving back from the color, see that color as the color of the person's dress or suit. If you like, the person can be standing with their back to you initially. Once you have moved back, got them in focus and are ready to begin, you can then get them to turn around. The tube imagery, with a color starting-point, can be a very useful introduction to clairvoyance.

At the conclusion of the sitting simply return to a single color, shorten the tube to its original size, and stand it back down on the floor in front of you. After a few moments of quiet you can open your eyes.

Fifth Exercise

Radiesthesia (the use of a pendulum for metaphysical purposes) can be extremely effective and I will deal extensively with it in later chapters on healing. As an introduction, however, try this simple exercise. Cut a strip of white paper, or cardboard, approximately twelve inches long and one inch wide. Color one end of the strip red, about two inches of it will do, and the other end blue. A two inch section in the center should be colored yellow.

If you have a pendulum, fine. If not then making one is very easy. Virtually any weight on the end of a string will do. A favorite is to loop a length of silk ribbon through a ring. Even a needle on the end of a thead will do. A neck-pendant on a fine chain is another possibility. The length of the thread/string/chain should be about seven to ten inches. Hold the chain between the thumb and forefinger so that, with the elbow resting on the table, the pendulum is suspended just above the table's surface. (Some radiesthesiatists suggest keeping the arm in the air, with the elbow *off* the table, but I have found no difference either way. Resting the elbow is certainly less tiring.) Use the right hand if right-handed, the left if left-handed.

Hold the pendulum so that it is suspended over the center of the red section of your strip of paper, as it lies on the table. Hold the chain still; do not consciously try to swing the pendulum. Do not grip too tightly. Now concentrate your thoughts on the color red. See a ball of red light at the end of the strip of paper. See it encompassing the pendulum. You will soon notice the pendulum starting to swing. It will swing more and more strongly moving in a circle, *clockwise* about the red area *(Fig. 6)*.

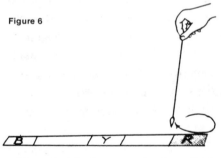

Figure 6

When it is swinging well, move your arm across so that the pendulum is now suspended over the blue end. See, here, a blue ball of light encompassing the pendulum. You will probably be surprised to find that the pendulum will slow, stop, and start to swing again in the opposite, *counterclockwise,* direction. As much as you change ends, and color concentrations, so will the pendulum change directions. If you stop it and then hold it over the center section, and imagine yellow. it will swing backwards and forwards along the line of the strip of paper.

You will get the same reactions from the pendulum if,

instead of simply imagining the appropriate colors, you concentrate your thoughts on those things associated with the colors (see *Color Chart* page 16). Over red, think of strength, health, vigor, etc. Over blue, think of tranquility, understanding, devotion. Over yellow: attraction, charm, confidence.

Sixth Exercise

Psychokinesis (PK) is the moving of material objects without physical contact. To demonstrate the "pressures" applied in PK we can perform a simple exercise using an animate object . . . a person. You will actually need a minimum of three people for this exercise (more than three is fine). On one side of the room sit one person (or group) that we will call A. On the other side of the room sit another person (or group) we will call B. Let a toss of the coin decide which will be Red and which Blue. For the first run let's say that A is Red and B is Blue.

Now bring in a person who has been kept outside while the coin was tossed. This should be a person who is fairly relaxed. Have him or her stand in the center of the room, at ease, with the legs slightly apart. Let's call this person X.

Groups A and B should now concentrate their thoughts on their respective colors. With eyes closed, they should see themselves surrounded by red or blue light and should see it extending out to touch X. (If there are several people, so that you have groups rather than individuals, then let one or two of each group concentrate on the associations *[Color Chart, page 16]* rather than on the actual color.)

What will (or should) happen now is that X will find him/herself being drawn towards the Red group—in this first run, A—and repelled by the Blue group. X will probably become aware of feelings of warmth and love coming from the Red group; coldness from the Blue. Do this experiment a number of times, flipping a coin each time to see which will be Red and which Blue. Do not, of course, let X know which is which. You will find that X will far more frequently be drawn to the Red than to the Blue. Question X after each run and get reactions.

Seventh Exercise

A simple, inanimate, exercise can be done using a corkball (easily obtained at fishing-supply stores). Tie a length of thread to a pin and then push the pin into the corkball. Hang the ball so that it is free on all sides.

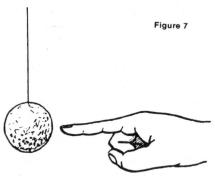

Figure 7

Point your fore-finger at the suspended ball, as close as you can without actually touching it *(Fig. 7)*, and concentrate your thoughts on the color blue. Feel the blue all about you; see it about and even within your body. Direct it down your arm and out of your finger. As you direct out the blue, so you should see the corkball move *away* from your finger.

Concentrate on red, and the corkball will swing *towards* you, actually hitting the tip of your finger. Experiment with other colors.

Eighth Exercise

Clairaudience is the ability to *hear* psychically. It may be accompanied by clairvoyance, but not necessarily so. How do we hear color? Through music.

Color and music share common terms. We speak of tone, pitch, intensity, and volume, for both arts. Chromatic is another common word. There is a psychological phenomenon whereby certain people subconsciously "see" colors in sounds. This is known as *color synesthesia.* Colors can even be brought about by sound. In the Los Angeles Times (December 3, 1948) there was an AP report on a machine known as an *Auroratone,* invented by an Englishman named Cecil Stokes. Musical vibrations registered on a sensitized emulsion and were photographed by a movie camera. A different pattern of color was created in the emulsion by each individual note. When projected, accompanied by the music, the result was a glorious series of color patterns subtly changing with the mood of the music. More recently a color organ has been developed, by Thomas Douglas Jones. Known as the *Chromaton,* it produces colored light as it is played.

Sir Issac Newton, three hundred years ago, related colors to the diatonic scale. C = Red; D = Orange; E = Yellow; F = Green; G = Blue; A = Indigo; B = Violet. Slow music is generally associated with the blue end of the scale, and fast music with the red end.

An interesting exercise towards clairaudience can be performed using a large conch shell. We are all familiar with the "sounds of the sea" that can be heard by holding such a shell to the ear; but more than the sea can be heard by the sensitive.

Sit comfortably, back straight, breathing exercises done, and hold the shell to your ear. You will first hear the familiar rushing sound but, if you concentrate, you may become aware of a subtle musical background sound. Concentrate on it and try to bring it out. In clairaudience a shell is often used, by a developing medium, to spark the initial contact and to focus the voice(s) being heard. If you can also pick up a musical accompaniment, as it were, then you can glean additional very useful information based on the tempo and pitch of the music, together with any repeated, emphasized, individual notes. This is not easy to do, admittedly, but you might take heart from the fact that some years ago Theodore F. Karwoski and Henry S. Odbert conducted a study* with 148 people, testing for color response to music. Of these, 60% did get a response of some kind (40% of these actually "saw" colors). If you get that sort of response then, again, refer to the color associations listed in *Color Chart* (page 16).

These are some simple exercises in psychic development associated with color. There are many more. Experiment yourself. Color can be a tremendously useful tool, as you will find more and more in succeeding chapters.

Always go through the breathing exercises before any experiment. In fact, it certainly won't hurt you to do a complete color meditation each time! And remember . . . practice makes perfect.

*Color-Music, Psychological Monographs Vol. 50 No. 2. 1938, Ohio State University, Columbus.

3

COLOR IN DIVINATION

There are many different methods of divination. Some people prefer cards, others crystal- or mirror-gazing, still others work with Numerology or the I-Ching. Over the centuries there has been an incredible variety of forms of divination, many with unpronouncable names: alectoromancy, astragalomancy, oneiromancy, moleosophy, tasseography, libanomancy, pyromancy, molybdomancy, cephalomancy, lampadomancy, and so on. But whatever the form, and whatever the label, there are really only two criteria: Is it accurate? Does it work for you?

To help you find a method that does work for you, and one which you will feel comfortable with, and especially to improve the accuracy, you can utilize the principles of color.

The actual basics of How to Divine (how to read the Tarot, how to crystal-gaze, how to work a pendulum, etc.) I have dealt with elsewhere* so, concentrating on the advantages of color in divination, let me start out here by first looking at the *place* of divination. Of course you *can* divine almost anywhere—spread out your Tarot cards in the sand at the

A Pocket Guide to the Supernatural Raymond Buckland. Ace Books, New York 1969.

beach, or throw the I-Ching sticks in the back of a pick-up truck—but if you are serious about this art, if you want to get the very best of results and get them consistently, then you will find it pays to be more selective.

The Divination Room

A Divination Room is the ideal; one set aside just for divining. This may be asking too much, however, particularly if you only have a two-room apartment! So the next ideal is the Divination Cabinet. Spiritualist mediums frequently operate from a curtained-off "tent" arrangement known as a Cabinet. It serves a very useful purpose in containing whatever energies are raised. A variation of the Spiritualist Cabinet can serve you, but where the medium's is invariably black yours will be colored. It is no coincidence, by the way, that many "fortune-tellers" at carnivals, in Gypsy tea-rooms, or working out of store-fronts, do their actual readings in colorful curtained-off areas.

The ideal Cabinet should be just large enough to contain two chairs and a card table. It should be roofed; the height no more than six feet. (It is not difficult to design a wooden framework that will fold down to handy carrying size, thereby making your Cabinet portable). The actual color(s) of the drapes enclosing the framework will be a matter of experimentation. The obvious choice would seem to be blue: tranquility, understanding, patience, truth, etc. *(Color Chart,* page 16), but there are other possibilities. You may find that the joy and comfort of yellow, or the stimulation and attraction of orange, or the power of violet, are more condusive to your doing readings. Why not a combination of colors? Two sides of blue, two of green, and a roof of yellow might be an ideal combination. I find that the cooler colors are more sympathetic to the wide variety of readings you are likely to encounter than are the hotter ones.

To find the best color(s) for you to work under, without spending lots of dollars on yards and yards of different materials, test yourself with colored lights. Do a few divinatory layouts in a blue light, then a few in a green light, and so on. Note that I say a few "layouts", not "readings". With many forms of divination—the Tarot is, perhaps, the most obvious—color plays a part in the interpretation. With everything bathed in a blue light, then, all your colors would be affected. So, at this stage, don't try to do any actual readings/interpretations, just get the feeling of working in that color light.

You will find that there are one, two, or perhaps three, colors which leave you far more relaxed than the others. Then this color/color combination is the one you will use to cover your Cabinet. It sets the right vibrations for you to work in. A candle, or desklamp, on the table can then take care of the illumination for the actual readings and so overcome the lighting problem mentioned above.

Now to specifics. How can color improve the accuracy of scrying? What does color have to do with Numerology? What color is the I-Ching? What about color and Palmistry? . . . there are many ways that color can improve these, and most other, forms of divination.

Crystal Gazing

Crystal-gazing, a branch of scrying, is a form of

divination that many people have trouble with. Usually it is just a question of practice, but many get discouraged before they achieve their first "vision".

Instead of just gazing into the crystal and hoping for something (anything!) to appear, start out with a definite objective in mind. Do your breathing exercises, as detailed in Chapter One (I would also recommend wearing the CM Robe, not only for this particular exercise but for all the experiments outlined in this book). Then sit quietly and focus your mind on what you would like to see. Perhaps you have a particular question you want answered, or a specific person you want to see. Boil down that question, or person, to a single point: an emotion, a feeling, an action, or whatever.

For example, you would like to meet with your recently deceased, greatly missed, Uncle Max. He was always a jolly person, full of vigor, seemingly healthy, which was why everyone was surprised when he suddenly dropped dead in the middle of the church picnic. "Vigor" would seem to sum up Uncle Max. Vigor = Red.

For a second example, you would like to find out whether the weekend meditation seminar you plan to attend will be beneficial and how it will affect you. This is basically a combination of tranquility/devotion and need for under-standing, all of which are allied with the color Blue.

Take the color you have arrived at and, in your mind, project it into the crystal-ball. See the ball full of that color (blue, or red, or whatever). *Don't* try to project Uncle Max himself in there, or a full weekend seminar. It would be too complicated and would defeat its own objective. No: just project the color. Proceed as normal and you will find that when the scene finally "breaks" it will be centered on the person/question you wanted.

If you have difficulty projecting a color into the ball with your mind, slip a small square of the appropriately-colored velvet, or silk, underneath the ball. With this method, however, you must remove the cloth once the imagery starts. Try to carefully slip the material out again from under the ball (and drop it on the floor, or put it behind you on the chair). Be warned, it will be difficult to do this without losing concentration and, hence, the whole picture (The reason the colored cloth must be removed is that the color permeation could interfere with other color information that is to come to you).

Much of what you see in a crystal (or in any other form of scrying: mirror-gazing, ink-blot, water, polished copper, etc.) is symbolic, as in most methods of divination. Pick up on colors as much as you can, and use the Color Chart, page 16, to help you interpret.

Numerology and Chromology

Numerology may seem a far cry from Chromology but the two can usefully be put together. The key is in the numerical value of the primary colors. They are as follows:

1 — Red
2 — Orange
3 — Yellow
4 — Green
5 — Blue
6 — Indigo
7 — Violet
8 — Rose
9 — Gold

To equate *seven* primary colors with *nine* primary numbers it is necessary to go into the higher octave for the colors, i.e. Rose is the higher octave of Red; Gold is the higher octave of Orange. Rose and Gold, then, have similar associations to those equated with Red and Orange in the Color Chart, (page 16). Rose = Strength, Love, Leadership, Judgement, Arbitration, Respect. Gold = Joy, Cheer, Hope, Happiness, Communication, Counseling.

From basic Numerology we have the numerical values of the letters of the alphabet:

1:	A	J	S
2:	B	K	T
3:	C	L	U
4:	D	M	V
5:	E	N	W
6:	F	O	X
7:	G	P	Y
8:	H	Q	Z
9:	I	R	

As an example let's look at ex-president Jimmy Carter through Numerology/Chromology. Remember that in Numerology you work with *the name most commonly used,* so it is Jimmy Carter, not James Carter.

```
J I M M Y     C A R T E R
1 9 4 4 7     3 1 9 2 5 9 = 54 = 9
```

Note the preponderance of 9's. There are three in the names and then the Name Number itself is a 9. By Numerology a 9 person is very emotional; active, though ruled by the emotions; tied very much to family background; impulsive. Okay. But what more can we learn by Chromology? Well, 9 is the number of Gold, and Gold means Joy, Cheer, Happiness (that ever-present, toothy, smile?), Hope,

Communication and Counseling.

You can go a step further. With the three 9's in the name there are also two 1's (Red) and two 4's (Green). This would then indicate Strength, Vigor, Charity; Growth, Energy, and Luck.

There is one further step you can take: what is lacking? All numbers are represented with the exception of 6 (Indigo) and 8 (Rose). We can ignore the absence of 8 since there are a couple of 1's, and we know that 8 is simply a higher octave of 1. So the only number/color totally absent is 6/Indigo, a color associated with Dignity. It might, then, behoove Mr. Carter to wear the color Indigo, perhaps in a tie, in order to give his appearance more dignity and generally round himself out chromologically. So, from this example, it can be seen that Chromology can indeed expand on basic Numerological insight.

Rolling Dice

A step along from Numerology is divining with dice. A very basic, simple method, useful to determine the outcome of events or the choice of a path to take, is to have the Querant roll a pair of dice. The resultant individual numbers, plus their sum, are then equated with colors as in Numerology.

For example, suppose the Querant wishes to know whether or not she should meet with a certain man on a particular weekend. She concentrates her thoughts on the question, as she handles the dice, then throws them down. Let's say they land showing a 2 and a 5. We know that 2 is Orange and 5 is Blue. The sum of the two numbers is 7 — Violet.

From Color Chart I you can interpret: Orange gives encouragement, stimulation, attraction. Blue shows understanding, devotion, sincerity . . . it sounds good for that weekend! Violet, the sum of the two, shows sentimentality but also tension, possibly sadness. From the positivity of the Orange and Blue you can probably ignore the sadness, or soft-pedal it. The tension is certainly understandable, and not necessarily a bad thing. To sum up, you could say that the weekend promises to be very productive. There will be good rapport, perhaps after an initial uneasiness.

This form of divination can, obviously, be expanded to other branches, such as dealing out playing cards, or overturning dominoes. The basic interpretation will rest on equating the resultant numbers with colors.

An expansion of the above would be a form of Astragalomancy. This was the name given to divining by a letter, or symbol, on each of twelve knucklebones thrown down on the ground. Variations are found all over the world: the natives in Nigeria use six carved pieces of wood; the Shoshone Indians use different shaped stones. Interpretation depends upon how and where the objects fall.

Take three wooden cubes, each about the size of a regular die. On each cube/die paint one side red, one side orange, one yellow, one green, one blue, and one violet.

The Querant places a coin on the ground, to represent himself. He then shakes up the three colored dice, concentrating his thoughts on his question. The dice are thrown down on the coin. Interpretation is of the resultant colors according to their relationship to the coin—the closer a color to the coin, the more powerful and immediate the force(s) affecting the individual. It will be found that many times two, or even all three, of the dice will show the same color, indicating very powerful and positive influences.

Tarot

When teaching the Tarot I have always emphasized that the Tarot cards should be interpreted according to the Reader's "feelings" rather than by reading-off specific meanings from a published book of "interpretations". If a particular card—let's say the Ten of Wands, for illustration—turns up in a particular position when you are reading for person A, then it has certain meanings for that person. But if that same Ten of Wands should show up in the same position in a reading for person B, then it is *not* likely to have the self-same meaning; for A and B are two separate and very distinct personalities. If you are reading from a book then the Ten of Wands means "overcoming a problem; sweeping away opposition; assertion", and that's all . . . whether it's for person A, person B, person C, D, E, or whomever. Throw that book away!

As you turn over each card your eyes will be drawn to a specific symbol, a particular part or aspect of the illustration, far more strongly than to any other part. This is the key to your interpretation—not what a book says.

Perhaps this is not the place to get into a complete How to Read the Tarot* but I want to bring out the point that your eye will not only be attracted by a particular object or

---

*A future title in this "Practical Magick Series" is *Practical Divination,* which will include detailed instructions on Tarot reading.

symbol, but also it will pick up one particular color more than the others. This "color consciousness" can be very useful in adding interpretations of what you see.

The Waite-Rider deck is an excellent one, and one I personally use regularly. When I wish to work more with Chromology in my readings, however, I find that the best is the Crowley-Thoth deck. Try this, concentrating on the color vibrations, and see what a lift it will give to your readings.

Color, then, can play a very useful part in divination. I have given some suggested uses; there are many more you will find for yourself.

Instead of throwing the I-Ching sticks (or coins) on a table or a rug, lay down a square of material of a color appropriate to the question being asked.

When reading palms, be aware of any warmth or coldness—especially at the fingertips and on the mounds—and equate these with the red and blue ends of the color spectrum.

In Radiesthesia, try using different colored pendula.

And so on . . . experiment for yourself.

4

COLOR IN MAGICK (i)

Aleister Crowley defined Magick as "the Art or Science of causing change to occur in conformity with Will." In simpler terms he was saying: "Make something happen that you *vant* to happen." That is Magick. I don;t think that definition can be bettered. Color Magick, then, is making something you want to happen do so, through the use of color.

What sorts of things do people want to happen? Well, we can usually divide up our wishes and desires under four main headings: Health; Wealth; Power; Protection.

Anything we desire, can be. Anything. The power is ours. Here follow, then, some simple rituals utilizing Color Magick, which can help us draw on our own powers to create our own realities. Work them in quiet solitude* when there is a real need (do not attempt Magick simply "to see if it will work"!). A word of caution—you can create your own reality,but don't do it by interfering with someone else's reality. An example would be love magick to influence a particular person. This should never be done, for it would be

---

*By which I mean cut off from the ordinary everyday world . . . preferably in a room kept aside solely for magickal purposes. The rituals themselves may be done by the individual or by a group.

interfering with their free will; forcing them to do something they wouldn't normally do, and might not want to do. The only sort of love magick that should be done is that aimed non-specifically . . . to bring *"someone"* to you, without knowing exactly who it will be. Far better to work on yourself, to make yourself generally more attractive, than to try to change someone else. So, always consider what effect your magick might have on others.

Incense should always be burned throughout the magickal ritual. Apart from helping give the right atmosphere, it is said that the smoke of the incense carries your prayers up to the Gods. Any pleasant-smelling incense will do. I would particularly recommend frankincense or sandalwood, but follow your own preference. Cones, stick, or powdered incenses are equally suitable.

Most magickal rituals are best performed after sundown but, again, choose the time most convenient for yourself. What matters is that you should be *comfortable* as you work. You should be comfortable as regards time, place (feeling that you will be completely free from any interruptions), and your dress. Again I would recommend the CM Robe, with nothing beneath it.

These rituals may be done for yourself or for another. In the rituals you will be using colored Plackets. *Placket* is the old English word for Pocket (it was also a slang term for the vagina!). These are simple pockets made by sewing together two rectangles of colored material, leaving one side open so

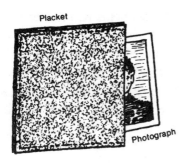

Placket

Photograph

Figure 8

that an object, such as a photo-graph, may be inserted *(Fig. 8)*. I made my Plackets of felt but silk, cotton, or just about any material will do. I have Plackets in each of the primary colors, plus one Healing Placket which is red on one side and green on the other, and others in combinations of colors (e.g. green and blue for "to bring good fortune"—see below).

A table-top, shelf, top of a chest-of-drawers, or whatever, can be set up as an Altar. On it you should have a religious figure/symbol/picture (if you so desire; this is optional), with a white Altar Candle on either side of it. Your Censer (incense dish) is in front of these. To the left and the right are your colored Ritual Candles (see below), with the Placket in between *(Fig. 9)*. For working the following rituals I have

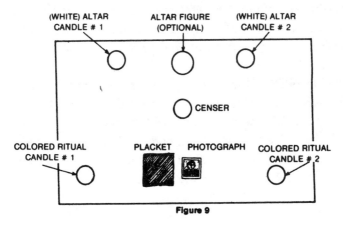

(WHITE) ALTAR CANDLE # 1   ALTAR FIGURE (OPTIONAL)   (WHITE) ALTAR CANDLE # 2

CENSER

COLORED RITUAL CANDLE # 1   PLACKET   PHOTOGRAPH   COLORED RITUAL CANDLE # 2

Figure 9

indicated that photographs of the Recipients be inserted in the Plackets. If a photograph is not available then use *any* representation of that person: e.g. an object belonging to the person that has been handled by them (such as a handkerchief); a specimen of their handwriting; a small Poppet*; or, if nothing else, their full name and birthdate written on a piece of paper.

★   ★   ★

To Bring Health to Someone Sick

(See also Chapters 6 and 7—Color in Healing.)
Ritual Candles #1 and #2 should be RED.
Placket should be RED and GREEN.

Light Altar Candles #1 and #2.
Light Incense.
Spend a few minutes in quiet meditation, preparing your mind for the ritual. If you wish, you may say the Lord's Prayer (or other, suitable to your persuasion).

PETITIONER   I am here to bring renewed health to . . .
SPEAKS: (Name) . . . Through the Powers that Be,
                working their will through me, I would
                bring about a body and mind fit and well;
                healed of all infirmities and happy and
                joyous in life and love.

---

*Magical Doll—see Chapter 5.

Light Ritual Candles #1 and #2.
Take up photograph of Recipient and hold it in the smoke of
the incense.

"Here is . . . (Name) . . . This is he/she.

Place the photograph in Placket and then hold Placket
between the palms of the hands. Concentrate your thoughts
on Recipient. See him/her well and happy*. See the Power
of Light—the Red light of Health and Strength, and the
Green light of Energy, Growth and Healing—flowing
down, through your body, and into the Recipient. Keep this
up for as long as you can concentrate, then lay the Placket
back down on the Altar.

Clear your mind and see, now, a ball of white light filling
the room, purifying everything and everyone within it.
According to your preference, you may say either the
Twenty-third Psalm or the Pagan Seax-Wica Psalm.

23rd PSALM
The Lord is my shepherd; I shall not want.
He maketh me to lie down in green pastures:
    he leadeth me beside the still waters.
He restoreth my soul: he leadeth me in the
    paths of righteousness for his name's
    sake.

---

*If the Recipient has a broken leg, see him running and jumping; if he has a sore throat, see him
shouting and singing; if a bad back, see him turning somersaults! In other words, see him in
perfect health. Not *getting* better, but *already* better.

Yea, though I walk through the valley of
the shadow of death, I will fear no
evil: for thou art with me; thy rod
and thy staff they comfort me.

Thou preparest a table before me in the
presence of mine enemies: thou an-
nointest my head with oil; my cup
runneth over.

Surely goodness and mercy shall follow
me all the days of my life:
and I will dwell in the house of the
Lord forever.

SEAX-WICA PSALM

Ever as I pass through the ways
Do I feel the presence of the Gods.
I know that in aught I do
They are with me.
They abide in me
And I in them,
Forever.
No evil shall be entertained,
For purity is the dweller
Within me and about.
For Good do I strive
And for Good do I live.
Love unto all things,
So be it, Forever.

Extinguish the candles—Ritual Candles first, then the

Altar Candles. Leave the photograph in the Placket. If the whole Altar set-up can be left intact, all the better. Leave until the same hour next day then, taking the photograph out of the Placket, repeat the entire ritual.

Repeat again on the third day, then leave the photograph in the Placket until the Recipient is completely well.

To Bring Good Fortune

(Note: Start this ritual on a Wednesday.)
Ritual Candles should be GREEN.
Placket should be GREEN and BLUE.

Light Altar Candles.
Light incense.
Spend a few moments in quiet meditation, preparing your mind for the ritual. If you wish, you may here say the Lord's Prayer (or other).

PETITIONER   . . . (Name) . . . has been as a stranger to
SPEAKS: Good Fortune. Whatever the reason may
                          it now be meet that the forces may change.
                          Let all that is good be his/her lot from
                          henceforth. Let new life flow that he/she
                          may partake of the joys and rewards of this
                          life, from this day forth.

Light Ritual Candles.
Take up photograph of Recipient and hold it in the smoke of the incense.

Here is . . . (Name) . . . This is he/she.

Place photograph in Placket and then hold Placket between the palms of the hands. Concentrate your thoughts on Recipient. See him/her happy and contented. See the Power of Light—the Green light of Luck and Good Fortune and the Blue light of Patience and Truth—flowing down, through your body, and into the Recipient. Keep this up for as long as you can concentrate, then lay the Placket back down on the Altar.

Clear your mind and see, now, a ball of white light filling the room, purifying everything and everyone within it. According to your preference, you may say either the Twenty-third Psalm or the Seax-Wica Psalm (see above). Then extinguish the candles—Ritual Candles first, then the Altar Candles. Leave the photograph in the Placket. Leave until the same hour next day then, taking the photograph out of the Placket, repeat the entire ritual.

Repeat again on the third day, then leave the photograph in the Placket for seven days.

To Bring Needed Wealth*

(NOTE: Start this ritual on a Wednesday.)
Ritual Candles should be ORANGE.
Placket should be GREEN.

Light Altar Candles.
Light incense.

---

*This ritual will not bring money just for the sake of having money. It will not keep you comfortably so that you won't have to work! *But* if there is a need—if you have done all you possibly can, and failed, then here is Magick "to bring needed wealth".

Spend a few moments in quiet meditation, preparing your mind for the ritual. If you wish you may say the Lord's Prayer (or other).

PETITIONER   Great is the need of . . . (Name) . . . He/she
SPEAKS: has striven and labored long and hard in
              search of that which is needed so desper-
              ately. The need is great; the desire is here.
              Grant that those forces which must come
              into play will do so, to bring about just
              ends for . . . (Name) . . .

Light Ritual Candles.
Take up photograph of Recipient and hold it in the smoke of the incense.

              Here do I present . . . (Name) . . .

Place photograph in Placket and then hold Placket between the palms of the hands. Concentrate your thoughts on Recipient. See him/her holding the necessary money in hand. See the Power of Light—the Green light of Finance—flowing down, through your body, and into the Recipient. Keep this up for as long as you can concentrate, then lay the Placket back down on the Altar.

Clear your mind and see, now, a ball of white light filling the room, purifying everything and everyone within it. You may say either the Twenty-third Psalm or the Seax-Wica Psalm (see above). Then extinguish the candles — Ritual Candles first, then the Altar Candles. Leave the photograph in the Placket. Leave until the same hour next day then, taking the photograph out, repeat the entire ritual.

Repeat again on the third day, then leave the photograph in the Placket for seven days.

To Bring Happiness

Ritual Candles should be ORANGE.
Placket should be YELLOW.

Light altar Candles.
Light Incense.
Spend a few moments in quiet meditation, preparing your mind for the ritual. If you wish you may say the Lord's Prayer (or other).

PETITIONER   I am here to help channel happiness to . . .
SPEAKS: (Name) . . . one who is presently without
                          that vivid spark of life. I would bring a
                          smile to his/her face and laughter to his/her
                          heart, in all that he/she might do.

Light Ritual Candles.
Take up photograph of Recipient and hold it in the smoke of the incense.

                          Here is . . . (Name) . . ., the one for whom
                          I speak.

Place photograph in Placket and then hold Placket between the palms of the hands. Concentrate your thoughts on Recipient. See him/her happy and and contented in all things. See the Power of Light — the Yellow light of Joy, Happiness and Comfort — flowing down, through your body, and into the Recipient. Keep this up for as long as you can concentrate, then lay the Placket back down on the Altar.

Clear your mind and see, now, a ball of white light filling the room, purifying everything and everyone within it. You may say either the Twenty-third Psalm or the Seax-Wica Psalm (see above). Then extinguish the candles—Ritual Candles first, then the Altar Candles. Leave the photograph in the Placket. Leave until the same hour next day then, taking the photograph out, repeat the entire ritual.

Repeat again on the third day, then leave the photograph in the Placket for nine days.

To Cause Love Between Two People
(NOTE: Start this ritual on a Friday.)
Ritual Candles should be RED.
Placket should be RED and ORANGE.

Light Altar Candles.
Light incense.
Spend a few moments in quiet meditation, preparing your mind for the ritual. If you wish you may say the Lord's Prayer (or other).

PETITIONER   Let the light of love pour forth equally
SPEAKS: between ... (Name) ... and another. I

am here to direct that light, in purity and
truth, that it might attract and seal them
together in perfect harmony of life and love;
heart to heart and mind to mind.

Light Ritual Candles.

*Take up photograph of the one seeking love and hold it in
the smoke of the incense.*

Here do I present . . . (Name) . . . who
would be as one with another.

*Place photograph in Placket and then hold Placket
between the palms of the hands. Concentrate your thoughts
on Recipient. See him/her with another, both together,
loving, happy, and affectionate. See the Power of Light —
the Red light of Love and Strength and the Orange light of
Attraction, Stimulation, Adaptability and Kindness —
flowing down, through your body, and into the Recipients.
Keep this up for as long as you can concentrate, then lay the
Placket back down on the Altar.*

*Clear your mind and see, now, a ball of white light
filling the room, purifying everything and everyone within
it. You may say either the Twenty-third Psalm or the Seax-
Wica Psalm (see above). Then extinguish the candles —
Ritual Candles first, then the Altar Candles. Leave the
photograph in the Placket. Leave until the same hour next
day then, taking the photograph out, repeat the entire ritual.*

Repeat again on the third day, then leave the photo-

graph in the Placket for twenty-one days.

To Bring Love to Fulfillment (Sex)
(NOTE: Start this ritual on a Friday.)
Ritual Candles should be RED.
Placket should be RED.

Light Altar Candles.
Light incense.
Spend a few moments in quiet meditation, preparing your mind for the ritual. If you wish you may say the Lord's Prayer (or other).

PETITIONER That the love which exists by . . . (Name)
SPEAKS: . . . should be brought to fruition is the
            desire of this Petitioner. I would bring
            about the physical union of these two
            people, in joy and in love; in trust and in
            devotion.

Light Ritual Candles.
Take up photographs of both Recipients* and hold them in the smoke of the incense.

> Here are . . . (Name) . . . and . . . (Name)
> . . ., to be brought together in the joys of love.

---

*If the Petitioner is actually one of the Recipients—i.e. if he (or she) is the one who wishes to consummate love with his partner—then he may work with just the photograph of this partner, visualizing her acceding to his desires.

Place photographs in Placket and then hold Placket between the palms of the hands. Concentrate your thoughts on Recipients. See them in the act of love. See the Power of Light — the Red light of Sexual Love — flowing down, through your body, and into the Recipients. Keep this up for as long as you can concentrate, then lay the Placket back down on the Altar.

Clear your mind and see, now, a ball of white light filling the room, purifying everything and everyone within it. You may say either the Twenty-third Psalm or the Seax-Wica Psalm (see above). Then extinguish the candles — Ritual Candles first, then the Altar Candles. Leave the photographs in the Placket. Leave until the same hour next day then, taking the photographs out, repeat the entire ritual.

Repeat again on the third day, then leave the photographs in the Placket for twenty-one days.

To Consecrate a Talisman*

NOTE: Start this ritual on the day appropriate to the purpose of the Talisman (e.g. Friday for a Love Talisman; Wednesday for a Money Talisman; Saturday for a Protective Talisman). *Ritual Candles and Placket should be colors appropriate to the purpose of the talisman—see Color Chart, page 16.*

Light Altar Candles.
Light incense.
Spend a few moments in quiet meditation, preparing your

---

*See Chapter 5 for instructions on making a Talisman.

*mind for the ritual. If you wish you may say the Lord's Prayer
(or other).*

PETITIONER   I am here to consecrate this Talisman. Let
SPEAKS: it be imbued with all the power I would
                       have it possess. Let that power be forever
                       with its bearer, focusing through this object
                       to enhance and magnify his/her natural
                       elements, wherein he/she may use it.

Light Ritual Candles.
Take up Talisman and hold it in the smoke of the incense.

                       By the smoke of this incense do I cleanse
                       this Talisman of all impurities, preparing
                       it for the reception of its own awesome
                       power.

   *Place Talisman in Placket and then hold Placket
between the palms of the hands. Concentrate your thoughts
on the talisman, seeing it as the holder of All Power for the
good of Love, Protection, Wealth, or whatever. See the
Power of the Light — the Red light of Love, Health, and
Strength (or, again, whatever color/attributes you are
working for) — flowing down through your body and into
the talisman. Keep this up for as long as you can concentrate,
then lay the Placket back down on the Altar.*
   *Clear your mind and see, now, a ball of white light
filling the room, purifying everything and everyone within
it. You may say either the Twenty-third Psalm or the Seax-*

Wica Psalm (see above). *Then extinguish the candles —*
Ritual Candles first, then the Altar Candles. Leave the
Talisman in the Placket. Leave until the same hour next
day then, taking the talisman out, repeat the entire ritual.

Repeat again on the third day, then leave the talisman
in the Placket for twenty-one days.

To Protect Against Evil

(NOTE: Start this ritual on a Saturday.)
Ritual Candles should be WHITE.
Placket should be BLUE and VIOLET.

Light Altar Candles.
Light incense.
Spend a few moments in quiet meditation, preparing your
mind for the ritual. If you wish you may say the Lord's
Prayer (or other).

PETITIONER   Evil shall not touch upon . . . (Name) . . .,
SPEAKS: for he/she shall be protected by the
              all- encompassing power of light. Let that
              light so shine that naught that is evil
              may enter the sphere of his/her being,
              but be rejected and sent into the everlasting
              darkness.

Light Ritual Candles.
Take up photograph of Recipient and hold it in the smoke of
the incense.

Here do I present . . . (Name) . . ., in purity.

Place photograph in Placket and then hold Placket between the palms of the hands. Concentrate your thoughts on Recipient. See him/her surrounded by the shining white light of Purity; ever protected from evil of any kind. See the Power of Light — the Blue light of Patience, Truth, and Devotion, and the Violet light of Power and Piety . . . see them both further enveloped in the great White light of Purity and Protection — flowing down, through your body, and into the Recipient. Keep this up for as long as you can concentrate, then lay the Placket back down on the Altar.

Clear your mind and see, now, a ball of white light filling the room, purifying everything and everyone within it. You may say either the Twenty-third Psalm or the Seax-Wica Psalm. (see above). *Then extinguish the candles — Ritual Candles first, then the Altar Candles. Leave the photograph in the Placket. Leave until the same hour next day then, taking the photograph out, repeat the entire ritual.*

Repeat again on the third day, then leave the photograph in the Placket for seven days.

To Drive Out Evil Infuences (Exorcise)
(NOTE: Start this ritual on a Saturday.)
Ritual Candles should be VIOLET.
Placket should be WHITE.

Light Altar Candles.
Light incense.
Spend a few moments in quiet meditation, preparing your

*mind for the ritual. If you wish you may say the Lord's Prayer
(or other).*

PETITIONER   I seek to cleanse and purify . . . (Name) . . .
SPEAKS: of aught that is Evil abiding within or
                about him/her. Let only Good enter in and
                let Purity abound. Drive out and exorcise
                those forces which are not One with the
                Light, that the Gods may hold true dominion
                over all.

Light Ritual Candles.
*Take up photograph of Recipient and hold it in the smoke of
the incense.*

                        Here is . . . (Name) . . . that I seek to purify.

*Place photograph in Placket and then hold Placket
between the palms of the hands. Concentrate your thoughts
on Recipient. See him/her in an attitude of prayer and
devotion, with white light radiating from within. See the
Power of Light — the white light of Purity, Goodness, and
Truth — flowing down, through your body, and into the
Recipient. Keep this up for as long as you can concentrate,
then lay the Placket back down on the Altar.*

*Clear your mind and see, now, a ball of white light
filling the room, purifying everything and everyone within
it. You may say either the Twenty-third Psalm or the Secx-
Wica Psalm (see above). Then extinguish the candles —
Ritual Candles first, then the Altar Candles. Leave the*

photograph in the Placket. Leave until the same hour next day; then, taking the photograph out, repeat the entire ritual.

Repeat again on the third day, then leave the photograph in the Placket for twenty-one days.

It can be seen that the above rituals may be adapted for many purposes. The basic, essential, parts are as follows: A statement of purpose; a cleansing and naming (in the incense); a concentration of Power, through the direction of (colored) light.

As with all Magick, we all have this power within us, to use as we will. Through the use of color take that power and direct it, working for the good of your fellow man and woman.

5

COLOR IN MAGICK (ii)

Magick is a practice. Anyone can do (or attempt to do) magick. That makes them a Magician. You don't have to be a Witch, or a practitioner of Voodoo, or an Oriental Master to do magick. Anyone can be a Magician. Of course, some are far more successful at it than others.

There are many different forms of magick . . . dozens, perhaps even hundreds. In the previous chapter we looked at just one — Placket Magick. An easy and safe method. Some of the others can be very dangerous. Ceremonial Magick, for example; where the Magician is conjuring and working with various entities, most of them decidedly antagonistic towards the Magician. Not only is this dangerous but, to my mind, the risks are totally unnecessary. It is a little like trying to hook up a 1,000 volt power line to run a transistor radio! Why take the risk when a simple little battery will do the job just as well and without the danger?

As I said at the start of Chapter Four, magick is making something happen that you want to happen. One of the ways to do that is by building power, within a consecrated circle, and then releasing it. The power builds up in the form of a cone and is, in fact, referred to as "the Cone of Power" in Witchcraft. Singing, dancing, chanting, physical activity (such as sex), can all be used as ways of cultivating that power. Here is where color can come in handy. Obviously in one chapter I cannot teach you all the intricacies of working the many different systems of magick, but I will try to show you how color can be advantageously employed in some of the systems.

COLOR CONE

To be an effective magical practitioner, you need to be well versed in the arts of meditation, concentration, and visualization. Before starting your magickal work, sit for a moment and meditate on what you wish to achieve. Then, visualize the circle filling with white light. See the light all around you, totally encompassing you. It will form around you and build up into the shape of a cone. This is the white light of protection. Now, once that is firmly there, gradually change that whiteness into a color — first of all a pale blue, for tranquility, understanding and sincerity. Then gradually darken the blue. Take it to indigo and then on through to a deep purple. You will by then feel that there is already power in the circle. Keep the purple for a few moments then, gradually, change the color to the one most suitale for the magick you are going to work. If you are going to do a healing then green might be appropriate (though, again, it will vary depending upon the type of healing). If you are working to bring money then orange, or gold, for attraction, might be appropriate. Working for love? A pink cone would be good. Now go on to do the ritual work; the raising of the power by whatever method.

COLOR CARRIER BEAM

When the time to release comes, again incorporate color. Instead of just releasing, and seeing the power fly from you to its target, send it in a beam of colored light. This would be the same color as that used at the finale of the opening cone (above) . . . green for healing, orange for money, etc. When the energy has gone and you have done all you can, then return to a white cone about you.

CANDLE MAGICK

While not the subject of this book, the burning of colored candles is one of the most effective ways of working magick. I have dealt fully with this in a companion volume to the present work — *PRACTICAL CANDLEBURNING RITUALS* (Llewellyn Publications, 1982). Candleburning is perhaps the easiest way for the beginner to get into the working of magick and, especially, to become familiar with the symbolism of colors. It is another version of sympathetic magic and, again, is a safe, basic form of magick.

POPPET MAGICK

A Poppet is a specially prepared cloth doll, that represents a particular person. The basis of Poppet magick is the sympathetic variety already discussed. Whatever you do to the doll, in ritual, you in effect do to the person it represents.

The color of the cloth you use for the doll is determined by the purpose of the Poppet. Many Poppets are made for healing purposes and there the cloth color will depend on the patient's problem. Refer to Color Chart (Chapter 2, page 16) to determine the color for your Poppet. You are wanting to get a new job? Why not use indigo, the color of ambition? You're trying to develop charm and confidence? Use yellow. You want to attract money to you? Do one side of the Poppet in orange (for attraction) and the other in green (for finance). Don't be afraid to have a multi-colored Poppet. And use as bright colors as you can.

From the cloth cut out two simple basic shapes *(Fig. 10)*. As you cut, concentrate on the person the doll is to represent. It doesn't have to look *exactly* like them when it's done, so long as you really concentrate and, to *you*, the Poppet actually becomes the person. Sew the two pieces of cloth together, leaving an opening in the top of the head *(Fig. 11)*.

Figure 10

Figure 11

Stuff the Poppet with suitable filling. If you are doing a healing then the appropriate herb should be used. If you're working for money, chop up some Monopoly money and stuff it with that. For love? Fill it with rose petals or confetti. Think about a good filling. See just how creative you can be. When filled, sew up the top of the head.

Figure 12

Now, again concentrating hard on the actual person, decorate the Poppet to look as much like the person as possible. Sew on colored wool (or real hair, if you can get it) to represent their hair. Embroider — or draw with felt-tip pens, if you're not very good with a needle — the facial features. On the body write their name and mark their astrological sun sign, moon sign, and rising sign, if known *(Fig. 12)*.

When writing the name, I suggest doing it in one of the traditional magickal alphabets and also doing it in the color appropriate for the person's birth date:

ARIES—Red	LEO—Orange	SAGITTARIUS—Purple
TAURUS—Yellow	VIRGO—Violet	CAPRICORN—Blue
GEMINI—Violet	LIBRA—Yellow	AQUARIUS—Indigo
CANCER—Green	SCORPIO—Red	PISCES—Indigo

There are a large number of magickal alphabets which can be found in such books as *THE KEY OF SOLOMON THE KING* (MacGregor-Mathers), *THE MAGUS* (Barret), and *CEREMONIAL MAGIC* (Waite). Here is one of the most popular, known as *Theban. (see Fig. 13).*

THE THEBAN ALPHABET

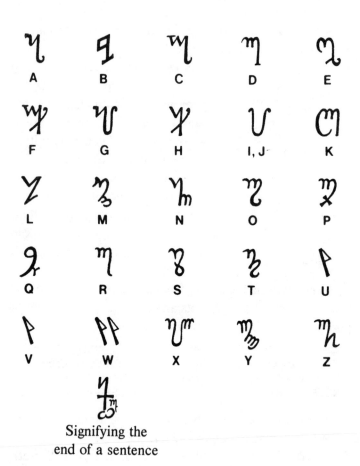

Signifying the
end of a sentence

Figure 13

When you have constructed your Poppet, and personalized it, then is the time to begin the actual magickal ritual. You should set up an altar, as described in Chapter 4, but with the Poppet lying where the Placket was. After lighting the candles and the incense, take up the Poppet and hold it over the altar. Say:

> Here is . . . (name) . . . This is her/him in every way. All that I do to this Poppet I do to her/him.

Hold the Poppet in the smoke of the incense and *see* the person it represents. Proceed then as you did for the Placket magick in Chapter 4, but using the Poppet instead of the Placket/photograph.

The advantage of Poppet magick is that you put so much of yourself, of your personal *power*, into the making of the Poppet that it becomes a very potent tool.

TALISMANS

A talisman is a man-made object endowed with magickal powers, especially for averting evil from, or for bringing luck to, its owner. In this sense a rosary, crucifix, St. Christopher medal, etc., are all talismans. But the most powerful magick is that done by the person affected. In the same way, the most powerful talisman is one actually made by the person who needs it. A talisman made by one person for another can never be as strong as a personally made one.

According to the magickal order, the Hermetic Order of the Golden Dawn, a talisman is "a magickal figure charged with the Force which it is intended to represent". It is so charged by (i) inscription, and (ii) consecration. It can be of any shape, but let us first look at the *material* of the talisman.

A talisman can be of virtually any material — paper, silver, copper, lead — but traditionally some substances are more appropriate than others and their use will imbue the talisman with more power. For example, as you know the days of the week are each ruled by a planet: Sunday — SUN; Monday — MOON; Tuesday — MARS; Wednesday — MERCURY; Thursday — JUPITER; Friday — VENUS; Saturday — SATURN. Now each of these planets is, in turn, associated with a metal: Sun — GOLD; Moon — SILVER; Mars — IRON; Mercury — MERCURY; Jupiter — TIN; Venus — COPPER; Saturn — LEAD.

From the table of correspondences used in candleburning magick, we know what properties are governed by the days of the week, and can therefore correlate those properties with the metals:

SUNDAY - Sun - GOLD - Fortune; hope; money
MONDAY - Moon - SILVER - Merchandise; dreams; theft
TUESDAY - Mars - IRON - Matrimony; war; enemies; prison
WEDNESDAY - Mercury - MERCURY - Debt; fear; loss
THURSDAY - Jupiter - TIN - Honor; riches; clothing; desires
FRIDAY - Venus - COPPER - Love; friendship; strangers
SATURDAY - Saturn - LEAD - Life; building; doctrine; protection

So, for example, knowing that Friday is associated with love (ruled by Venus) and that the metal is copper, we now know that a love talisman, for greatest effect, should be made of copper.

Mercury gives a bit of a problem in that it is a liquid metal. It could be used by containing it in a miniature bottle, or similar, of some other metal, but it is more usual — and a lot easier — to substitute either gold, silver, or parchment. Today, also, many substitute aluminum. Parchment, gold or silver can likewise be used in place of *any* of the other metals if they are unobtainable, but obviously the specified metal would be the best.

Having chosen your metal, what should you inscribe on it? There are many talismanic designs shown, in occult books, taken from such old grimoires as *The Greater and Lesser Keys of Solomon, The Black Pullet, Le Dragon Rouge,* and similar. But just copying these designs, without knowing their meanings or significance, and without personalizing them, is completely useless. You need to work specifically for your problem. The most common form a talisman takes is a metal disc worn on a chain, as a pendant. On one side of the disc place the personalization and on the other side the objective. Let's do an example.

Jane Doe wants to get married. She already has a boyfriend, so love is not what she is seeking. Looking at the Table of Correspondences, we see that Mars rules *matrimony.* That's what she needs — a talisman to bring matrimony. The metal for Mars is iron. Jane can either obtain an iron disc and engrave on it, or she can opt for the easier gold, silver, or parchment.

She is going to personalize one side of it. She will do this by putting her name and date of birth on it. She can use one of the magickal alphabets for the name. She can also add her astrological sun sign, rising sign (ascendant) and moon sign, plus ruling planets. These can all be arranged on the disc. There is no special pattern that has to be followed; anything aesthetically pleasing will do. Figure 14 gives two possible

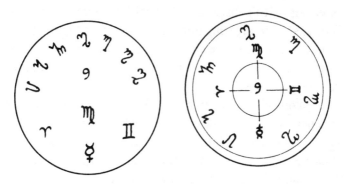

Figure 14

alternatives. Each has the same symbols, but in different arrangement.

As each of the symbols is engraved, or drawn, Jane should concentrate on herself, seeing herself as she best likes herself — charming, happy, self-confident. On the reverse side of the talisman she should put symbols traditionally associated with marriage: wedding bells, flowers, rings, hearts, etc. Or, she could place a *sigil* constructed from numerological squares, as follows.

4	9	2
3	5	7
8	1	6

Figure 15

From numerology (Chapter 3) we know that the numerological value of the word "matrimony" is $4+1+2+9+9+4+6+5+7 = 47 = 11 = 2$. You now construct a Magick Square (More on *Magick Squares,* generally, below) containing all the numbers one through nine *(Fig. 15).* Now, starting at the first letter (M = 4) draw a small circle, to indicate the start, and then draw a line to the second letter/number: A = 1. Follow on to 2 and then to 9. There are two nines in the word so stop-and-start there with small triangles: $>\!<$ Continue through to the last letter and draw another small circle to indicate the end.

At square 2, the numerological total (47 = 11 = 2), draw a large square. The finished figure will look like figure 16–A. Transfered off the squares, it will look like figure 16–B.

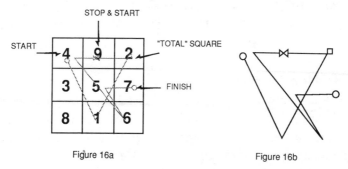

Figure 16a   Figure 16b

What you see in 16–B, then, is the sigil for matrimony. Jane can inscribe this on the reverse of the talisman. As she does so, she should concentrate her thoughts on the marriage itself; see herself as a bride, see herself and her husband wearing wedding bands, see the ceremony taking place, etc. . . . Such a sigil would be far more potent than the traditional bells, hearts, and rings, of course. Incidentally, the Magickal Square used is the ancient Chinese "Square of Lo Shu" and is the best for constructing sigils based on numerology.

The day associated with matrimony was Tuesday. Then that is the day on which Jane Doe should make her talisman. She should also choose a Tuesday that is in the waxing phase of the Moon.

Whatever the purpose of the talisman, follow the same procedure: FIND THE DAY AND THE METAL ASSOCIATED WITH YOUR DESIRE; PERSONALIZE ONE SIDE OF THE APPROPRIATE METAL; TAKE THE KEY-WORD AND, FROM THE MAGICK SQUARE, FIND THE APPROPRIATE SIGIL; IN-SCRIBE THE SIGIL ON THE REVERSE, CONCENTRATING AS NECESSARY; FINALLY CONSECRATE THE TALISMAN (AGAIN DURING THE WAXING OF THE MOON) BY WASHING IT IN SALT-WATER AND HOLDING IT IN THE SMOKE OF INCENSE.

Now, for extra potency, use color on your talisman. One way is simply to always make your talisman on parchment and use colored inks for marking it. Use the color associated with the person's sun sign, for writing their name and personal symbols. On the reverse, use the color associated with the *day* for marking the sigil:

Sunday — YELLOW   Monday — WHITE   Tuesday — RED
Wednesday — PURPLE   Thursday — BLUE   Friday — GREEN
Saturday — INDIGO (or BLACK)

So, going back to Jane Doe's matrimony talisman, if she is a Virgo then she would write her name and other personal data in VIOLET and, on the reverse, draw her sigil in RED (red for Tuesday, the day for matrimony). If you want to stick with metal talismans, of course, there is no reason why you shouldn't paint the markings on, in the appropriate colors.

To finish off, instead of hanging the talisman on a chain, around your neck, hang it on a double length of colored thread or silk — the two colors used in the marking.

MAGICK SQUARES

Magick Squares are found in many parts of the world at different times. Basically they are talismanic figures. The best known, and perhaps most varied, collection is to be found in *THE BOOK OF SACRED MAGIC OF ABRA MELIN THE MAGE,* translated by S. L. MacGregor-Mathers. The Squares consist of letters arranged to form the square, though numbers can also be used. Probably the oldest example is found in China as "the Square of Lo Shu" *(Fig. 17).* It consists of the numbers one through nine arranged in such a way that they add up to fifteen in all directions — horizontally, vertically, and diagonally. This particular square is also found in Qabalistic writings as the Square of Saturn (there are Squares for each of seven planets).

Using color, and constructing them carefully, Magick Squares can be very potent talismans in themselves. Some of the more common ones are shown in figure 18.

IMPORTANT RULES TO FOLLOW WHEN WRITING-IN THE SYMBOLS (numbers or letters):

(i)   The symbols should all be of the same size.

(ii)   They must *not* touch the lines (which should be perfectly drawn).

(iii)   You must not allow your shadow to cover the Square as you work on it.

(iv)   The symbols must be written in their sequence.

(v)   You must concentrate on the purpose of the talisman as you construct it.

(vi)   Be absolutely confident of the success you will achieve.

For (iii) work facing the sun. This way your shadow won't fall completely over the Square, so long as you are careful. For (v) visualize the *end product.* For example, if

4	9	2	=15
3	5	7	=15
8	1	6	=15

15   15   15 = 45

45... 4 + 5 = 9

Figure 17

N	A	S	I
A	P	I	S
S	I	P	A
I	S	A	N

For Scrying

H	O	R	A	H
O	S	O	M	A
R	O	T	O	R
A	M	O	S	O
H	A	R	O	H

To Discover
Any Magick

D	A	C	A	D
A	R	A	F	A
C	A	M	A	C
A	F	A	R	A
D	A	C	A	D

To Bring Food
and Drink

S	E	A	R	A	H
E	L	L	O	P	A
A	L	A	T	I	M
R	O	T	A	R	A
A	P	I	R	A	C
H	A	M	A	C	S

To Recover
Something Lost

O	R	I	O	N
R	A	V	R	O
I	V	A	V	I
O	R	V	A	R
N	O	I	R	O

To Bring Money

S	I	T	U	R
I	R	A	P	E
T	A	R	A	G
U	P	A	L	A
R	E	G	A	N

For Health

S	A	L	O	M
A	R	E	P	O
L	E	M	E	L
O	P	E	R	A
M	O	L	A	S

For Love Of
a Female

D	E	B	A	M
E	R	E	R	A
B	E	R	E	B
A	R	E	R	E
M	A	B	E	D

For Love Of
a Male

Figure 18

C	A	R	A	C
A	R	I	O	A
R	I	R	I	R
A	O	I	R	A
C	A	R	A	C

To Discover Thefts

57	78	29	70	21	62	15	54	5
6	38	79	50	71	22	63	14	46
47	7	39	80	31	72	23	55	15
16	48	8	40	81	32	64	24	56
57	17	49	9	41	73	33	65	25
26	58	18	50	1	42	74	34	66
67	27	59	10	51	2	43	75	35
36	68	19	60	11	52	3	44	76
77	28	69	20	61	12	53	4	45

MOON: WHITE

6	32	3	34	35	1
7	11	27	28	8	30
19	14	16	15	23	24
18	20	22	21	17	13
25	29	10	9	26	12
36	5	33	4	2	31

SUN. YELLOW

4	14	15	1
9	7	6	12
5	11	10	8
16	2	3	13

JUPITER: Success
BLUE

2	9	4
7	5	3
6	1	8

SATURN:
BLACK/INDIGO

8	58	59	5	4	62	63	1
49	15	14	52	53	11	10	56
41	23	22	44	45	19	18	48
32	34	35	29	28	38	39	25
40	26	27	37	36	30	31	33
17	47	46	20	21	43	42	24
9	55	54	12	13	51	50	16
64	2	3	61	60	6	7	57

MERCURY: PURPLE

22	47	16	41	10	35	4
5	23	43	17	42	11	29
30	6	24	49	18	36	12
13	31	7	25	43	19	37
38	14	32	1	26	44	20
21	39	8	33	2	27	45
46	15	40	9	34	3	28

VENUS: GREEN

working to cure a sore throat, see yourself shouting and singing. If working to get a job, see yourself *in* that job, working and happily employed.

Concentrate on what you are doing, as you work on the Square, not allowing any interruption.

Before starting on the construction, it is a good idea to meditate on what you want. In making the Square, first consider its purpose. Let's use the Health Square as an example. Suppose you want a talisman to wear or carry to *retain* good health. Here blue would be a good basic color. So make the Square on blue paper (a good quality, fairly thick, paper is recommended). Red is the color of blood; also the color for health and strength. A good, vibrant, red ink, then, would be a good choice for the inscription. In red, draw the lines and write-in the numbers or letters.

Make sure the lines are carefully drawn and that all the letters are of uniform size, not touching the lines. Put them in, concentrating on your good health the whole time.

When using a Square with letters rather than numbers, use one of the magickal alphabets. Example: The Square to obtain the love of a woman, with the letters in Theban: *(Fig. 19)*.

Remember that colors are important. They make the Square far more potent than if it

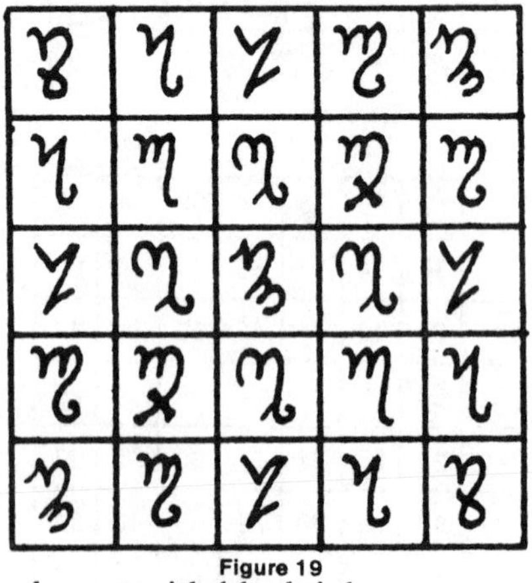

Figure 19

was just done on plain parchment with black ink.

6

CHROMOTHERAPY
COLOR IN HEALING (i)

In this and the following chapter I will deal with the use of color in healing. *I must make a point of saying that the information given is the result of my own personal research into the history of this use and it in no way reflects any engagement, on my part, in rendering professional medical advice. Such advice should be sought from a competent professional person.*

In this present chapter I will look at the use of color in such techniques as color projection, color breathing, and auric healing. In Chapter 7 I will detail hydrochromopathy, graphochromopathy, gem therapy, and therapy through music and sound.

COLOR PROJECTION
The most effective way to use color for healing — in fact, altogether the most effective form of chromotherapy — is *Chromopathy*... COLOR PROJECTION. This has been known for centuries. The ancient Egyptians and, before them, the Atlanteans used it, though it then fell into disuse until it was rediscovered at the beginning of this century. In

recent years it has grown into a rapidly developing serious study, recognized and utilized especially in Europe and the Far East.

As I mentioned in the Introduction to this book, our bodies select from sunlight whatever colors they need for balance. But we can boost this process by first determining what color(s) we are lacking and then giving ourselves a concentrated "shot" to supplement the sunlight.

The best way to get the different colors is by projecting light through filters, or *gels*—the colored sheets of gelatine and cellulose-acetate used in theatrical lighting. I use a product called "Roscolene," put out by the Adams Lighting Company (33 Bristol St., Cambridge, MA 02141). It is available in a wide variety of colors (approximately eighty), though you can start with the seven basics. It comes in sheets 20″ x 24″. Some researchers have found the use of colored silk placed in frames to work well. Dr. George White suggests that a good grade manufactured under the trade name *Faile-Matines* is suitable. Whatever you use, the idea is to project the suitably colored light onto the body of the patient for a certain period of time, allowing the body (or specific part of the body) to absorb it.

The simplest way to utilize the color sheets is to cover a window with the appropriate color* and then sit in the light of it. The only problem here is that you need a sunny day for it to work well and, for best results, there should only be one window in the room and for that to be completely covered with the color (if more than one window, then all should be completely covered with the color).

---

* I'll be detailing what colors to use for what, later in this chapter.

Equally effective, yet far more adaptable, is the use of a projector of some sort, in lieu of sun through a window. The projector can be set up anywhere and focused either on the entire body or just on a specific part. The light source, you see, does not have to be the sun . . . artificial light will work as well, though incandescent is preferable to fluorescent.

You can fasten a sheet of colored gel over a regular lamp— a gooseneck desk lamp is good–and use that. Or you can use a photographic slide projector. Buy a box of blank slide frames (usually cardboard or plastic), as used for mounting 35mm color transparencies, and fit a rectangle of colored gel in each. You can then use them in the projector and focus either on the body as a whole or on one particular section. I use a Kodak *Carousel* projector.

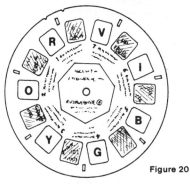

Figure 20

For working on small areas, I use a number of *gaf Viewmaster* projectors (model 300M). You may remember *Viewmaster* from your younger days, when you would drop a cardboard disc into the binocular-style viewer and look into it to see pictures in three dimensions. Well, in addition to the hand-held viewers, the *gaf* company produces small projectors for their series of discs. These projectors do not give a stereo effect, however, simply projecting a single one of each of the two coupled transparencies on the disc. What I did was to carefully remove the photo-transparencies from a disc — one from each of the pairs was all that was necessary *(Fig. 20)* —

and replace them with colored gels. I then had one disc with seven of my working colors on it.

PROPERTIES OF COLORS

For a complete listing of which color can be used for what, it would take a complete book in itself. Dinshah P. Ghadiali, a pioneer in chromopathy, gives the following general breakdown, in his excellent work *SPECTRO-CHROME HOME GUIDE* (Malaga, NJ 1933). I consider it one of the best.

RED

SENSORY STIMULANT – an agent that increases the activity of the sensory nervous system, energizing the senses of vision, smell, taste, hearing and touch.
LIVER ENERGIZER – an **agent** that activates the liver. *Use on area 7 (Fig. 21).*
IRRITANT – an agent that irritates.
VESCICANT – an agent that blisters.
PUSTULANT– an agent that suppurates.
RUBEFACIENT – an agent that reddens the skin.
CAUSTIC – an agent that burns and corrodes.
HEMOGLOBIN BUILDER – an agent that builds the coloring matter of the red blood corpuscles, in the liver. *Area 7.*

ORANGE

RESPIRATORY STIMULANT – an agent that increases breathing. *Areas 4-5-17.*
PARATHYROID DEPRESSANT – an agent that diminishes the functional activity of the four parathyroid glands, embedded in the right and left thyroid glands. *Area 3.*
THYROID ENERGIZER – an agent that increases the functional activity of the thyroid glands. *Area 3.*
ANTISPASMODIC – an agent that relieves spasm or sudden, violent, involuntary, rigid contraction due to muscular action.
GALACTAGOGUE–an agent that increases the secretion of milk after childbirth, by stimulating the mammary glands.*Areas 4-5.*

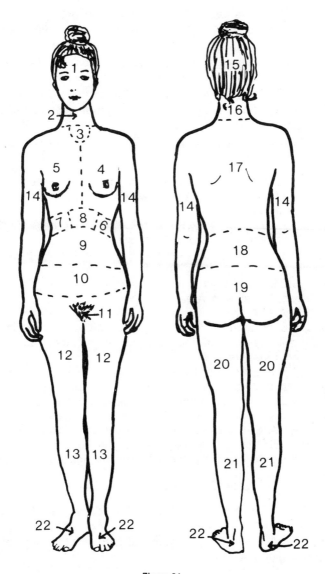

Figure 21

ANTIRACHITIC – an agent that corrects rickets or bone softness.
EMETIC – an agent that induces orelim (oral elimination) or vomiting, by irritating. *Area 8.*
CARMINATIVE – an agent that relieves flatulence or distension of the stomach or intestines with gases. *Areas 8-9.*
STOMACHIC – an agent that tones the stomach. *Area 8.*
AROMATIC – an agent that induces the qualities of spices. A stimulant.
LUNG BUILDER – an agent that builds the lungs. *Areas 4-5-17.*

YELLOW

MOTOR STIMULANT – an agent that increases the functional activity of the motor nervous system which energizes the muscles into motion.
ALIMENTARY TRACT ENERGIZER – an agent that activates the food passages. *Areas 8-9-10-18-19.*
LYMPHATIC ACTIVATOR– an agent that increases the functional activity of the lymphatic glands for nutrition.
SPLENIC DEPRESSANT – an agent that decreases the functional activity of the spleen. *Area 6.*
DIGESTANT – an agent that aids the process of converting food into materials fit to be absorbed and assimilated in the physical body, by stimulating the gastric and intestinal glands and pancreas. *Areas 8-9-18.*
CATHARTIC – an agent that produces increase in backelim (back elimination) or quickens purgation. *Areas 9-10-18-19.*
CHOLAGOGUE – an agent that accelerates the flow of bile. *Area 7.*
ANTHELMINTIC – an agent that is destructive to worms.
NERVE BUILDER – an agent that builds the nerves, by stimulating the choroid gland for cerebro-spinal fluid secretion. *Area 15.*

LEMON

CEREBRAL STIMULANT – an agent that increases the functional activity of the brain. *Areas 1-15.*
THYMUS ACTIVATOR – an agent that increases the action of the thymus gland. *Areas 4-5.*

ANTACID – an agent that neutralizes or counteracts acidity.

CHRONIC ALTERATIVE – an agent that produces a favorable change in the processes of nutrition and repair, in persistent disorders.

ANTISCORBUTIC – an agent that corrects scurvy, a disorder of nutrition and dietetic errors.

LAXATIVE – an agent that mildly loosens the intestines. *Areas 9-10-18-19.*

EXPECTORANT – an agent that promotes the ejection by spitting of mucus or other fluids from the lungs and windpipe. *Areas 2-4-5-17.*

BONE BUILDER – an agent that builds the body skeleton.

GREEN

PITUITARY STIMULANT – an agent that increases the functional activity of the pituitary gland in the head. *Area 1.*

DISINFECTANT – an agent that destroys rotting materials.

PURIFICATORY – an agent that purifies.

ANTISEPTIC – an agent that prevents decay.

GERMICIDE – an agent that kills germs.

BACTERICIDE – an agent that destroys micro-organisms or bacteria.

DETERGENT – an agent that cleans.

MUSCLE AND TISSUE BUILDER – an agent that builds muscles and tissues.

TURQUOISE

CEREBRAL DEPRESSANT – an agent that decreases the functional activity of the brain. *Areas 1-15.*

ACUTE ALTERATIVE – an agent that produces a favorable change in the processes of nutrition and repair, in recent disorders.

ACID – an agent that neutralizes or counteracts an alkali.

TONIC – an agent that tones the general system.

SKIN BUILDER – an agent that builds the skin.

BLUE

ANTIPRURITIC – an agent that prevents or relieves itching.

DIAPHORETIC – an agent that encourages perspiration.

FEBRIFUGE – an agent that dispels or reduces fever.

COUNTER-IRRITANT – an agent that allays irritation.
ANODYNE – an agent that soothes suffering.
DEMULCENT – an agent that allays the irritation of abraded or scratched surfaces.
VITALITY BUILDER – an agent that builds the life principle, by stimulating the pineal gland. *Area 1.*

INDIGO

PARATHYROID STIMULANT – an agent that increases the functional activity of the four parathyroid glands, embedded in the right and left thyroid glands. *Area 3.*
THYROID DEPRESSANT – an agent that decreases the functional activity of the thyroid glands. *Area 3.*
RESPIRATORY DEPRESSANT – an agent that decreases breathing. *Areas 4-5-17.*
ASTRINGENT – an agent that causes contraction and arrests discharges.
SEDATIVE – an agent that allays activity and excitement.
PAIN RELIEVER – an agent that allays suffering.
HEMOSTATIC – an agent that checks the flow of blood.
INSPISSATOR – an agent that dries or thickens.
PHAGOCYTE BUILDER – an agent that builds cells which destroy harmful micro-organisms.

VIOLET

SPLENIC STIMULANT – an agent that increases the functional activity of the spleen. *Area 6.*
CARDIAC DEPRESSANT – an agent that decreases the functional activity of the heart. *Area 4.*
LYMPHATIC DEPRESSANT – an agent that decreases the functional activity of the lymphatic glands for nutrition.
MOTOR DEPRESSANT – an agent that decreases the functional activity of the motor nervous system, which energizes the muscles into motion.
LEUCOCYTE BUILDER – an agent that builds the white corpuscles in the spleen. *Area 6.*

PURPLE

VENOUS STIMULANT – an agent that increases the functional

activity of the veins.

RENAL DEPRESSANT – an agent that decreases the functional activity of the kidneys. *Area 18.*

ANTIMALARIAL – an agent that prevents or removes malaria.

VASODILATOR – an agent that causes expansion of the blood vessels, lowering the blood pressure.

ANAPHRODISIAC – an agent that decreases sexual desires.

NARCOTIC – an agent that produces stupor.

HYPNOTIC – an agent that induces sleep.

ANTIPYRETIC – an agent that lowers the body temperature.

ANALGESIC – an agent that decreases sensitivity to pain.

MAGENTA

SUPRARENAL STIMULANT – an agent that increases the functional activity of the adrenal glands on the kidneys. *Area 18.*

CARDIAC ENERGIZER – an agent that increases the functional activity of the heart. *Area 4.*

DIURETIC – an agent that increases or promotes the secretion of frontelim (front elimination).

EMOTIONAL EQUILIBRATOR–an agent that stabilizes the emotions.

AURIC BUILDER – an agent that builds the aura or the radio-emanations of the chemical body.

SCARLET

ARTERIAL STIMULANT – an agent that increases the functional activity of the arteries.

RENAL ENERGIZER – an agent that increases the functional activity of the kidneys. *Area 18.*

GENITAL EXCITANT – an agent that stirs the functional activity of the genital organs. *Area 11.*

APHRODISIAC – an agent that arouses the sexual desires. *Area 11.*

EMMENAGOGUE – an agent that stimulates the ovelim (ovarian elimination) or menstruation.

VASOCONSTRICTOR – an agent that causes contraction of the blood vessels, raising blood pressure.

ECBOLIC – an agent that causes or accelerates expulsion of a fetus.

LENGTH OF TREATMENT

Project the color for *at least* thirty minutes each day. I find that most practitioners in fact treat for one thirty-minute period in the morning and then a second thirty-minute period in the evening.

DAYS TO TREAT

An essential part of life is rhythm. Undoubtedly a woman's menstrual cycle is one of the best recognized rhythms. It is (on average) a twenty-eight day cycle. Many women find a change in their moods within a week or ten days before the onset of their period, so there is nothing new to the observation of a twenty-eight day periodicity to emotions. And I'm sure everyone has noticed that they have "good" days and "bad" days.

Around the turn of the century (1895-1902) Herman Swaboda, professor of psychology at the University of Vienna, became interested in the rhythmic cycles of humans and detailed a twenty-three day cycle in certain aspects of illness. He considered this a masculine rhythm, in contra-distinction to the woman's twenty-eight day rhythm. He was, however, very much aware of the bisexuality of humans — each having component parts of the opposite sex in their make-up. Some years later, in the 1920's, Alfred Telscher, an engineering instructor, noted that his students' high and low peaks had a thirty-one day periodicity.

There are, then, three basic human rhythms. They are referred to as *Biorhythms:* a Physical twenty-three day cycle; an Emotional twenty-eight day cycle; an Intellectual thirty-three day cycle.

For over twenty years physicians and psychologists

observed and charted these changes. They observed that
these patterns covered these three main aspects and that
each rhythm never varied. Thus it was possible to *forecast*
good days and bad days; high energy days and low energy
days. And, most importantly, the "critical" days . . . the
days when most accidents occur, when you are most likely to
make poor decisions, and when you are most vulnerable to
illness. These are days when the physical and emotional
curves pass closely together from the positive phase of the
graph into the negative phase *(Fig. 22)*. As professionals in

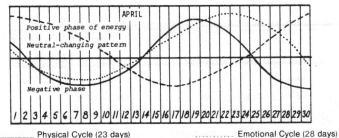

_____ Physical Cycle (23 days)   .... Emotional Cycle (28 days)
                         ---------- Intellectual Cycle (33 days)

Figure 22

Europe took up and furthered this study it was observed that,
by taking advantage of these circadian rhythms, surgeons
could cut down on post-operative complications and, for
example, on their critical days airlines and buslines could
keep pilots and drivers off duty.

        You can use these rhythms in the healing process, for
an individual's personal biorhythm can be more important
than the phases of the Moon. For example, if you are
working to aid in the mending of someone's broken limb,
working in the waxing phase of the Moon would be good,
but working when the person's individual physical biorhythm

was on the increase would be much better.

How do you find the individual's cycles? You can obtain tables to help you compute the rhythms, and instruments (such as *Biomatre)* to do it for you. Mathematically, you need to add up the total number of days in an individual's life, from the date of birth to the first day of the particular month for which the chart is to be constructed. This total is then divided by 23, 28, and 33 respectively. These divisions indicate how many times each cycle has run a complete span. The remainders show the position of each rhythm on the first day of the month being studied. It is obviously far easier to use a set of tables or a calculator, so I will not pursue the calculations here. On the subject of biorhythms I particularly recommend George S. Thommen's book, IS THIS YOUR DAY? (Crown, NY, 1973).

When working with chromopathy, then, it is good to have a copy of the patient's biorhythm and to plan the color treatments so that they take place when his/her Physical Cycle is on the increase (if you are working on a mental problem, then when the emotional Cycle is on the increase).

DIET

Along with the projection of color should go careful attention to diet, and even here you can be guided by color. For example, when the subject requires RED it is a good idea to incorporate into his/her diet such items as beetroot, red cabbage, radishes, red currents, red plums, etc.

For ORANGE: carrots, pumpkins, rutabagas, oranges, apricots, tangerines, peaches.

For YELLOW: Golden corn, parsnips, yams, sweet

potatoes, honeydew melons, pineapples, bananas, lemons, grapefruit.

For GREEN: Green vegetables and fruits that are not too alkaline or acid in their chemical reaction.

For BLUE: blueberries, damsons, blue plums, bilberries.

For INDIGO: as for Blue and for Violet, alternating.

For VIOLET: purple broccoli, beet tops, grapes, blackberries.

COLOR BREATHING

This is something that can be done at the same time as color projection yet, if necessary, can also be done quite separately, at any time and in any place.

When working with projected colored light, it is advantageous to visualize the very air itself as being colored and hence to *breathe in* that colored air. Working with, for example, a blue light, the subject breathes deeply and "absorbs" the blue into his/her body. He feels it filling his lungs and permeating throughout his entire body, reinforcing the action of the light on the outer surface. A suggested regimen, at that time, is the breathing exercise detailed in Chapter One, but very consciously and deliberately breathing in "colored air" throughout the exercise.

For a general tonic and rejuvenator it is a good idea, at least once a week, to breathe in the seven main colors in turn and use them to cleanse the chakra centers. It can be done as part of one of your regular meditation periods. Here is the best way to do it.

Sit as previously described, in Chapter One, but when you come to directing the Cone of Color to each specific chakra *(Fig. 3),* go a little further than that. Direct the color through the cone — let's use the green as an example — and also breathe it in through the nose and send it down to the thymus; to the heart area. But not only see/feel it absorbed into that area, see and feel it *swirling around,* very fast, in a clockwise direction. Keep it swirling and spinning, as fast as you can, for at least one full minute, then let it slow and stop. Pass on, then, to the thyroid and do the same thing with blue; breathing it in and directing it through the cone. Swirl it around the throat chakra rapidly for a full minute, then slow and move to the pineal (I used green as an example, to start, but you would normally start with the perineum — red, of course, and continue through all seven).

One of the joys of color breathing is that it can be done any time and anywhere, with no equipment. For example, suppose you have a touch of rheumatism in your left hand. While you are sitting watching television (or while you are driving to work, or *any* where or time), you can breathe deeply and see/believe/know that you are breathing in *blue* air. Breathe deeply and direct that blue air through your body to your left hand.

If you have difficulty visualizing a stream of blue air coming into you, then think first of yourself being completely surrounded and enclosed in a ball of blue light. Everything about you is blue. Then, as you breathe, you can't help but breathe in blue air. Now as you breathe and direct it to your hand, breathe in deeply and *hold the breath* for as long as you can. As you are holding it see, in your mind's eye, the hand loose and free and completely without the rheumatism.

This is a very important part of color breathing for

health. In addition to breathing in the appropriate color, *hold your breath for as long as you can and visualize the END product* — see the cure affected. If you are breathing cobalt blue for laryngitis, see yourself shouting and singing; if you are breathing red for asthma, see yourself breathing deeply and freely and unrestrictedly; if you are breathing green for a broken leg, see yourself running and jumping; if you are breathing yellow for constipation, . . . well, you get the idea!

A lady named Yvonne Martine, of Indiana, came up with the idea of breathing pink and directing it to her face to erase wrinkles and maintain her beauty. Needless to say, it worked. Many people have since tried it with amazing results. When I first heard of it I decided to experiment myself. Whilst driving to and from work each day I would spend ten minutes breathing pink and directing it to my face. I kept this up for a year. Today I am invariably taken to be anywhere from ten to fifteen years younger than my actual age!

If should be needless to say that with color breathing results are not instantaneous. Indeed it can take a very long time for it to have effect — though it *will* have effect. Color breathing is best used as a supplement to direct light chromology, or to the other therapeutic uses of color detailed in this and the next chapter.

AURIC HEALING

The body of Wo/Man is actually composed of seven distinct elements. The first three (solid, liquid, and gas) form the physical body. The fourth element is called the *Etheric* body and interpenetrates the physical. Generally the etheric body extends beyond the confines of the physical body by about an inch. Next is the *Astral* body. It extends several inches beyond the etheric body. Then, beyond the astral body, are the Mental and Spiritual bodies. Due to their elasticity, and the speed at which they function, it is impossible to define physical limits to these last two *(Fig. 23)*.

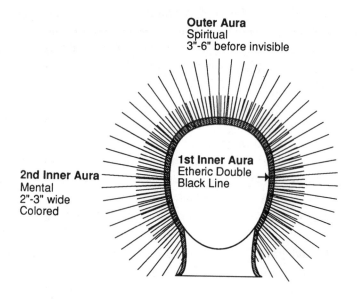

Outer Aura
Spiritual
3"-6" before invisible

2nd Inner Aura
Mental
2"-3" wide
Colored

1st Inner Aura
Etheric Double
Black Line

Figure 23

Although the vibrations of the non-physical bodies are too high a rate to be detected by the physical eye, the energy patterns that emanate can be seen by the adept. These energy patterns are what is known as the Aura.

Usually the energy of the etheric body is detected, or "seen", first because of its denseness. As your perceptions improve you can begin to detect the energy that radiates beyond the etheric body. Often it can be seen flowing, ebbing and spiralling, much like the Northern Lights. The colors detected are usually indicative of the person's state of being. Thus, a person with a deeply spiritual state may exhibit blue and lavender. A person deeply in love may show pink, etc. You should be cautioned about trying to see what another person sees, however. If you and a friend are reading auras, don't be surprised if one of you detects blue and the other detects yellow. Neither of you is necessarily wrong. Individual sensitivities are different and you are more sensitive to certain vibrations while your friend is more receptive to others.

Any state of the individual's being causes reactions in the aura. Emotional states will primarily affect the color. Physical conditions not only affect color but also cause peculiarities in the patterns of the aura, such as vortexes, holes, and sometimes dark spots. You should be careful in your treatment of information concerning auras. You may think that someone has a physical problem because of what seems to be a defect in their aura. Ask him if he has a problem in that particular area. But, if he denies it, drop the issue. What may appear serious to you at the time, could be just a minor irritation that is nearly healed. Remember the power of suggestion is strong and could turn out to be very damaging to some people.

The aura is sometimes referred to as "the odic force". In Christian art, from the fifth to the sixteenth centuries, it was

Figure 24

often depicted around the heads of people believed to possess great spiritual power. There it was referred to as *Halos* or *Glorias*. Around the heads, in paintings of Moslem prophets, it appears as a ring of flames. Crowns and Priests' headdresses symbolize the aura *(Fig. 24)*. In sculpture, Michaelangelo's statue of Moses depicts him with horns...which mystifies many. The reason is that in translation the word for *horns* was confused with the similar word for *rays* (of light).

In 1858 Baron Karl von Reichenbach, an industrial chemist, claimed to have discovered certain radiations coming from magnets, crystals, plants, and animals, which could be seen and felt by certain people (sensitives). In 1911 Dr. Walter Kilner, of St. Thomas' Hospital, London, devised ways of showing these radiations. One way was by looking through a dilute solution of a dye called DICYANIN (a product of coal-tar), and the other was by first looking at a bright light through a strong alcoholic solution then looking at the subject. This last method, however, proved to be very dangerous, causing damage to the eyes. Kilner did perfect his dicyanin method and produced what is known as the "Kilner Screen".

But the aura is best seen without artificial aid. Have your subject stand against a DARK background and look, directing your gaze at the position of the subject's third eye (between, and a little above, the eyebrows). You may find it helpful to squint slightly at first. You will become aware of the aura around his/her head though, at first, when you try to move your gaze to look directly at it . . . it will disappear! Don't worry. You will eventually be able to study it directly but, to start with, just keep your focus on that third eye and look at the aura peripherally. If you have no success with the subject against a dark background, then try a light background; some have success with one, some with the other.

The aura will be most obvious around the head, unless the body is naked in which case it will be seen clearly all around. The entire aura is called the *Aureole;* the head aura is the *Nimbus.* You may notice that to the person's *left* there is a generally orange color, and to their *right* a bluish color. If you move your hands towards the body you will feel warmth on their left and coolness on their right. Interestingly a bar magnet gives corresponding sensations, with the North end cool and blue and the South warm and orange. *(Fig. 25).*

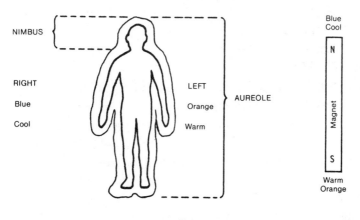

Figure 25

The aura can be felt. If you stand in front of your subject, with your hands extended on either side of his head, and the palms in towards him, you can feel it. Gradually move your hands in towards the head. As you approach (perhaps about four to six inches away) you will feel a tingling sensation, or a warmth, or a feeling of pressure building up. Move your hands in and out and get that sensation.

Auric healing is when the condition of a person is changed by the healer visualizing him/her surrounded by a specific color light.

For the NERVOUS SYSTEM, the auric colors used in mental concentration, are Violet and Lavender for soothing effects; Grass Green for invigorating effects; and Yellows and Orange for inspiring effects.

For the BLOOD and ORGANS OF THE BODY, Clear Dark Blues are soothing; Grass Greens are invigorating; and Bright Reds are stimulating.

For CASES OF FEVER, HIGH BLOOD PRESSURE, or HYSTERIA, think Blue.

For CASES OF CHILL, or LACK OF BODILY WARMTH, think Red.

So, for example, if a person is complaining of feeling hot, has a fever, and is sweating profusely, you can help immeasurably by concentrating on seeing him completely surrounded by, and absorbed in, a blue light. If he has a stomach pain, then direct a soothing light-green color to that area. For someone with a nervous headache, see their head surrounded by violet or lavender light. Keep this up for as long as you can. For a bleeding, direct clear dark blue light to the cut.

Keep up these visualizations for as long as you can, in each case. Then, finish them off with a pure white light projection. One of the advantages of auric healing is that it can be done without the subject's knowledge. The subject may not believe in it; may not want your help; may not understand what you want to do. But also he/she will not know when you are mentally projecting healing auric color waves at him/her.

7

CHROMOTHERAPY
COLOR IN HEALING (ii)

One of the exciting things about chromotherapy is that it can be used in so many different ways. In the last chapter, I spoke of color projection, color breathing, and auric healing. Now I'll look at healing with color-charged water, distant or absent healing through photographs, the healing properties of precious and semi-precious stones, and the healing power of sound.

HYDROCHROMOPATHY

Many psychic healers will take a glass of water and, cupping it in their hands, "charge" it with their healing powers. It is then given to the patient to drink. This practice can be expanded by charging water with *color*; something anyone can do.

By keeping your eyes open and checking antique stores, flea markets, garage sales, swap meets, etc., it is possible to obtain a collection of glass bottles, each in one of the seven main colors. The colors should be as "true" as possible (see *Introduction* regarding wavelengths). If you cannot get

colored bottles — or until such time as you can — you can use a clear glass bottle and fasten a colored gel around it *(Fig. 26)*.

The bottle is filled with water and stood in the window to absorb the light rays through its color (be it glass or gel). The water should preferably be pure spring water. Failing that, distilled water will do. Again, projected artificial light will do in place of sunlight, but it is certainly easy enough to simply stand the bottle in the window since there is no need for *direct* sunlight to shine on it . . . it can sit there on a cloudy day and still absorb. It should be in the window for at least an hour (three hours on a cloudy day) before using, and actually can be left there all day.

Feeling "down"; sluggish; no energy? Charge the bottle with RED and then drink a wineglassful of it three times a day. You'll be surprised how the red-charged water will pick you up. It's a great tonic.

Figure 26

Hot and feverish? Try some blue-charged water; again a wineglassful three times a day. Green-charged water is a very good general tonic.

Just be guided by the same principles used in color projection. In fact it's a good idea to supplement your chromopathy (color projection) treatment with the hydrochromopathy (color-charged water). One of the joys of hydrochromopathy is that it is so cheap . . . and it doesn't call for a prescription!

GRAPHOCHROMOPATHY

One of the oldest forms of magick is that termed *sympathetic* magick. To quote from my book *WITCH-CRAFT FROM THE INSIDE* (Llewellyn Publications, MN, 1975):

> Similar things, it was held (in Palaeolithic times) have similar effects; like influences like. Magick was used to direct the hunt. One man would represent the God and supervise the magick ... A model of the animal to be hunted was made, in clay, on the floor of the cave and, under the priest's direction, was attacked by the men of the tribe. Successful in 'killing' the clay animal the men could then go about the real thing confident that the hunt would go exactly as acted before the God.
>
> Evidence of this early religio-magick has been found in such places as the Caverne des Trois Freres at Ariege, France. Here can be seen the cave-painting known as *The Sorcerer*. This shows a man dressed in the skin of a stag and wearing a mask and horns. In Dordogne is found another such figure wearing the horns of a bull, and playing some form of musical instrument. At le Tuc d'Audubert, Ariege, is a very realistic clay model of a bison. It is pock-marked with holes where it was literally attacked with spears and javelins. There is also a similarly holed model of a bear. The bear has been modelled without a head, but possesses a hole in the neck which originally held a stake from which was hung a real bear's head. On a reindeer horn found at Laugerie Basse there is carved a prostrate man creeping up, on all fours, towards a grazing bison.

These actions, paintings and carvings, show how acting on a *representation* of a thing can actually effect the *real* thing. Taking it a step further, to a more modern example — albeit looking at a negative magick example — a Black Magician might take a photograph of his intended victim and stick it with pins, thus inflicting severe pain on the actual victim.

If the photograph can be used for evil ends, then it can just as easily be used for good purposes. By projecting color on to a photograph we can *sympathetically* project that color on to the person shown in the photograph, and thus can promote healing in that person.

The first thing needed, of course, is a good clear photograph of the patient. He, or she, should be the only one in the photograph and the area to be healed should be both plainly visible and not covered by clothing. Obviously the larger and clearer the photograph, the better. You can fasten the picture to a wall and use your projector to direct color on to it if you wish. Much easier, however, is to simply lay a sheet of the appropriately colored gel over the picture and stand it in the window. You can cut the gel to size and put it in a frame with the photo, if you prefer.

Once again, rather than sunlight you can use artificial light. Bill Finch, of St. Louis, MO, designed a clear "chromo-light" unit, with a holder for the photograph and filter, and a low-watt bulb as the light source. It has reflective material on the inside top and sides. Incorporating a time switch, you could set up one of these units to switch on and off regularly (as I have done) and give constant treatments to the patient via his/her photograph.

One advantage of graphochromopathy is that you can affect healing when the patient is not present, and even when the patient is at a very great distance. It will take much longer to have effect than direct treatment, of course, but over a period of time can be very beneficial. It is recommended to expose the photograph to the light for periods of at least an hour each, three times a day. The colors you use, of course, are the same as those you use for direct color projection.

GEM THERAPY

The simplest way to use precious and semi-precious stones is to be guided by their colors. You have a sore throat? Wear a necklace of sapphires (or blue semi-precious stones). Asthma? Wear a pendant of orange sardonyx, or of amber, next to the skin. Rheumatism or arthritis in the hand? Rings of orange sardonyx or amber and blue sapphires on the fingers will help. Heartburn? A pendant of yellow opal.

Here is a list of gems and stones together with their colors and properties.

AGATE - a banded, or irregular variegated, *chalcedony,* or crystalline quartz. Basically browns. Supposed to be good for the vision and also for hardening gums.

AMBER - fossilized resin, known variously as *burmite, pimetite, puccinite,* and *ruminite.* Good for throat problems, asthma, catarrh, also for aiding kidneys and liver.

AMETHYST - *quartz;* Its color may be due to traces of manganese; can be anything from bluish-violet to deep purple in color. Traditionally sobers the drunk, but also good for expelling all types of poison and generally toning the body.

BERYL - can appear white, yellow, green or blue. Good for liver complaints.

BLOODSTONE - or *heliotrope,* is the *plasma* variety of quartz. It contains small spots of red jasper, though it is basically green (from bright green to dark leaf green). Excellent for stopping bleeding and hemorrhages. Perfect for nosebleeds.

CARNELIAN - *chalcedony,* or quartz. Properties similar to Bloodstone. A blood purifier.

CHRYSOLITE (or *Peridot*) – *olivine;* usually olive green but sometimes yellow, brown, or even red. The greens and yellows will prevent fevers. Also said to prevent nightmares.

CORAL – *calcium carbonate* (skeletons of marine organisms). Both red and white coral prevent bleeding. Also said to avert the "evil eye". Frequently hung about the necks of children for general good health. Good for scars and ulcers.

CRYSTAL – colorless quartz, or rock crystal. A symbol of purity and great spiritual protector.

DIAMOND – considered something of a panacea, diamonds are especially good for coughs and mucus problems.

EMERALD – green variety of *beryl*. An antidote for poisons and very good for any diseases of the eyes.

GARNET – A deep red, good for the heart and as a general stimulant.

JADE – The green is a soothing, healing color. It is good for eye problems, kidney and urinary problems, and helps strengthen muscles.

LAPIS LAZULI – *lazurite,* ranges in color from rich azure-blue through violet-blue to greenish-blue. Good for eye problems. Very strong; should be used for short periods only.

LAPIS LINGUIS – *azurite;* various shades of blue. Good for meditating, and for bringing out your psychic abilities.

LAPIS LINGURIUS – *malachite;* bright green. A protection from the "evil eye". Also good for rheumatism and cholera.

MOONSTONE – *adularia* variety of *orthoclase.* Pearly opalescent, similar to an opal. As the Moon rules the water, so does the Moonstone govern affectations of a watery nature.

OPAL – a noncrystalline form of quartz; a silica gem containing varying amounts of water. There is what is termed "precious" opal, "fire" opal, and "black" opal. The precious opal contains a wide variety of delicate colorings; blue, green, yellow, and pink being especially noticeable. Fire opal, as its name suggests, is predominantly red though it can vary to honey-yellow with glimpses of red. Black opal has a dark green background with black flecks. Pliny described the opal as "made up of the glories of the most precious gems ... amongst them is the gentler fire of the ruby, the rich purple of the amethyst, the sea-green of the emerald, glittering together in union indescribable." Opals are especially good for use on children, perhaps because of their delicate colors. The opal has been called "the gem of the Gods", and is a stone of love . . . unless the lover be false, then — beware! It is often used for mental illness.

PEARL – a concretion formed by a mollusc. The Hindus listed the pearl as one of the five precious stones in Vishnu's magickal necklace (the other four were diamond, emerald, ruby, and sapphire). It has always been considered a cure for irritability. It is an ideal jewel to use in conjunction with another colored stone; the pearl adding its soothing qualities to the other's healing.

RUBY – *corundum;* a deep red in color, the ruby is especially connected with the blood and with the red end of the spectrum. Good for chills and lack of body warmth, poor circulation, constipation, ulcers, boils and biliousness.

SARDONYX – *cryptocrystalline quartz.* Different colored layers, mainly clear to brownish red along with white, brown, and black. Good for hemorrhages but mainly used for emotional states.

TOPAZ – an *alumino-fluoro-silicate;* a mineral of granites and other igneous rocks. Usually brown, yellow or pink (there is also a "false topaz" that is a brownish quartz). Used for soothing and calming, especially good for banishing nightmares and curing insomnia.

TURQUOISE – *copper-and-aluminum phosphate.* Light to dark blue, blue-green and green in color. For general healing. Good for lowering fevers and for calming nerves.

In her book *Healing and Regeneration Through Color* (New Age Press, CA, 1976), Corinne Heline gives the following tables of correlation for metals and precious stones with days of the week and astrological signs.

SUNDAY	Gold and Yellow gems
MONDAY	Pearls and all white stones
TUESDAY	Rubies and all red stones
WEDNESDAY	Turquoise, Sapphire and blue stones
THURSDAY	Amethyst and purple stones

FRIDAY   Emerald and green stones
SATURDAY   Diamond; also black stones

	Jewel	*Metal*	*Color*
ARIES	Ruby, Bloodstone, Red Jasper	Iron	Red
TAURUS	Golden Topaz, Coral, Emerald	Copper	Yellow
GEMINI	Crystal, Carbuncle, Aquamarine	M'cury	Violet
CANCER	Emerald, Moonstone	Silver	Green
LEO	Ruby, Sardonyx, Amber	Gold	Orange
VIRGO	Pink Jasper, Turquoise, Zircon	M'cury	Violet
LIBRA	Opal, Diamond	Copper	Yellow
SCORPIO	Agate, Garnet, Topaz	Iron	Red
SAGIT.	Amethyst	Tin	Purple
CAPRICORN	Black-and-White Onyx, Beryl, Jet	Lead	Blue
AQUARIUS	Blue Sapphire	Lead	Indigo
PISCES	Diamond, Jade	Tin	Indigo

MUSIC AND SOUND

In the case of a tuning fork vibrating in the air, the air is alternately compressed and rarefied by the action of the prongs, and the waves that are sent out consist of a series of alternate compressions and rarefications. The number of vibrations made in one second by such a sounding body is called the frequency. The human ear can perceive sounds only within certain limits of frequency: as low as 30 and as high as 24,000.

Color is to light what pitch is to sound. Color depends on the number of waves which strike the eye per second; pitch depends on the number of waves striking the ear per second. In color we have seven main colors. In music there are seven notes on the diatonic scale. The two have been equated, showing that every note gives off a color:

Middle	C	Red
	D	Orange
	E	Yellow
	F	Green
	G	Blue
	A	Indigo
	B	Violet

Just as you can supplement chromopathy with hydro-chromopathy, so you can also further (or alternatively) supplement it with *audio*chromopathy . . . have sound/-music to accompany your light treatments. For example, if you are projecting yellow light on to the stomach area, for constipation, then throughout the treatment a repeated sounding of the note E (yellow), or the playing of music which has the E especially predominant, can be highly beneficial.

When working with the chakras *(Color Breathing,* Chapter 5), it can be very useful to tie-in the sound of the specific note with each chakra color. One way, of course, would be by chanting on that note.

The constant repetition of one note can become weari-some, if not quite aggravating, however. It's therefore worth looking a little deeper into the audio side of chromopathy.

Taking the semitones into consideration (sharps and flats) we actually have *twelve* notes . . . the twelve semitones of the chromatic scale. These have been tied-in to the astrological sun signs to give "Keynotes" for each sign:

ARIES	D-flat major
TAURUS	E-flat major
GEMINI	F-sharp major
CANCER	G-sharp major
LEO	A-sharp major

VIRGO	C major
LIBRA	D major
SCORPIO	E major
SAGITTARIUS	F major
CAPRICORN	G major
AQUARIUS	A major
PISCES	B major

Each of the sun signs, in astrology, is equated with a specific part of the body:

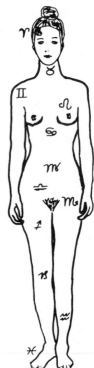

ARIES – Head, Ears, Eyes, Nose,
    Subrenal glands
TAURUS – Neck, Throat, Organs
    of Speech, Thyroid gland
GEMINI – Lungs, Arms, Shoulders,
    Nerves
CANCER – Breasts, Stomach, Ali-
    mentary canal
LEO – Heart, Spine, Back
VIRGO – Intestines, Nervous
    System
LIBRA – Kidneys
SCORPIO – Sex organs
SAGITTARIUS – Liver, Hips,
    Thighs
CAPRICORN – Knees, Bones,
    Teeth
AQUARIUS – Ankles, Shins,
    Circulation
PISCES – Feet.

You can see, then that when working on a particular part

of the body you can arrive at the correct Keynote through astrological correlation. To use the example, from above, of working for the problem of constipation, this would be the intestinal area which is governed by Virgo. Virgo's Keynote is C major. So any piece of music in the key of C major would be fitting accompaniment for the color therapy for constipation. Another example . . . working on the kidneys — kidneys are ruled by Libra. The Keynote for Libra is D major, so any piece of music in the key of D major would be good here.

As you can see, all the Keynotes given are majors. It should be noted that where the problem being treated is a mentally-related one, the *minor* key is better. The major keys have been described as "outpouring, productive and expanding". The minor keys as "secretive, sustaining, and enfolding".

In *Healing and Regeneration Through Music* (New Age Press, CA, 1978), Corrine Heline gives a partial list of musical "prescriptions" used by Harriet A. Seymour, of the Music Division of the Hospital Visiting Committee of New York:

> Of benefit to persons suffering from paralysis and disorders of the joints: Sousa's marches, *The Anvil Chorus, William Tell Overture,* Brahms' *Hungarian Dances, By the Waters of the Minnetonka.*
>
> Of benefit to persons afflicted with tuberculosis: Strauss' waltzes, *La Paloma, Minuet in G,* Schubert's *Serenade, March of the Wooden Soldiers,* Brahms' *Lullaby,* Schubert's *Ave Maria, From the Land of the Sky Blue Water, Somewhere Over the Rainbow.*
>
> Beneficial to persons being otherwise treated for heart trouble: The *Barcarolle, The Blue Danube,* Chopin's *A Minor Waltz,* Tango music, *Humoresque,* Cui's *Orientale, Song of India, Donna é Mobile,* Oley Speake's *Sylvia.*
>
> For persons suffering from insomnia and from pain generally: Mendelssohn's *Spring Song, Meditation From Thais,* Chopin's

Preludes, On Wings of Song, Andante, Beethoven's *Fifth Symphony, Adagio,* Beethoven's *Pathetique Symphony.*

For soothing persons suffering from certain mental and nervous afflictions: Rhythmic folk songs, *County Derry,* songs of Stephen Foster, Spanish tangoes, Brahm's *Hungarian Dances,* Sousa's marches, Strauss' Waltzes, Gilbert and Sullivan, *Indian Love Call, My Wild Irish Rose, Wishing, Estrellita.*

RADIESTHESIA FOR DIAGNOSIS AND PRESCRIPTION

Radiesthesia is a science related to dowsing or divining. We have discussed the fact that all matter vibrates, radiating energy. Ellic Howe says *(Man, Myth, and Magic,* V. 17, Marshall Cavendish, NY 1970):

> Consider two concepts: first, that all matter radiates on its own wavelength; and second, that living organisms, meaning human beings, animals and even plants, emit electromagnetic wave radiations which depend for their intensity and frequency upon general vitality and metabolism, and in the case of human beings, and perhaps even animals, on psycho-physical tone. Thus given the identification of a 'wavelength' that appears on the basis of past experience to reflect some kind of pathological or psychical imbalance, the radiesthetic practitioner will attempt to correct the imbalance.

The pendulum is the instrument of the radiesthetic. In Chapter Two I introduced you to its use in psychic development. The electrical field that emanates from the body has both a positive and a negative charge. When a pendulum is held over the positive (usually on the right side of the body), it swings in a clockwise direction. When held over the negative (left side), it swings in a counter-clockwise direction. The size of the circle in which it swings is indicative of the strength of the field. The pendulum is actually one of the most sensitive of all divining instruments and is especially suited to precise work such as medical diagnosis and treatment. This is especially recognized in Europe where medical radiesthesia is burgeoning.

DIAGNOSIS

In radiesthetic and radionic practice there are ten general disease conditions considered. These are:

1: VIRUS	6: SECRETION IMBALANCE
2: BACTERIUM	7: HORMONE IMBALANCE
3: POISON	8: MINERAL IMBALANCE
4: ALLERGY	9: VITAMIN IMBALANCE
5: TOXINS	10: PSYCHOLOGICAL CONDITION

Make up a 3″ x 5″ card with these ten conditions on it, in the form of a semi-circle *(Fig. 27)*.

To diagnose yourself, simply sit and concentrate on yourself, asking yourself what the condition is. Then hold the pendulum

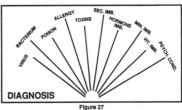

Figure 27

over the card and, as you keep asking, you'll see it start to swing strongly to one of the ten listed conditions. If you are diagnosing someone else, hold their right hand (left, if left-handed) in your free hand and ask the pendulum about *their* condition. If the person you wish to enquire about cannot be present, you can get the result by simply holding something beonging to them . . . a bloodspot on a piece of paper; saliva sample in a phial; item of personal clothing; used handkerchief; even a good photograph (of the person alone).

To be more specific in your diagnosing you can make up additional cards, each for one of the ten main groups, but with the particular condition broken into specifics (*i.e.* a list of viruses; a list of allergies; etc.). The pendulum you use for diagnosis, and for treatment (see below), should be one with a long, thin point to it, for accuracy.

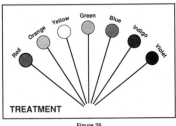

Figure 28

TREATMENT

Another card will display the seven main colors, either by color or by word *(Fig. 28).*

The swing of the pendulum will indicate the needed color to treat the ailment. Watch the pendulum carefully here. It may swing *between* two of the main colors, indicating an intermediate shade. Here again you could have secondary cards, one for each of the main colors, but shading gradually through to the next color on either side of it.

Another possibility is that the pendulum will swing first on one color and then on a second. This would be an indication of the need for both of those colors in the treatment.

I would recommend one more card, for daily treatment 1 time. This is especially useful if you find that more than one color is needed, since it will give the times for each — one color may be needed for the majority of the treat-

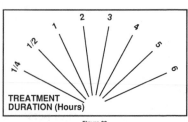

Figure 29

ment time with the second color as a minor supplement *(Fig. 29).*

8

COLOR IN EVERYDAY LIVING

How drab our lives would be without color. Contrast looking out of your window on a dull, rainy, misty morning in the fall or winter with looking out on a bright, sunny morning in the spring or summer. The one makes you want to withdraw and seek inner warmth and brightness; the other gives you a feeling of expansion, of well-being, and positivity. The colors in Nature are so noticeable: the bright greens of grass and darker greens of leaves, the brilliant yellows of dandelions and buttercups, the bright blue of the sky . . . In our homes we use color to brighten our lives. We paint and paper the walls of our rooms, carefully choose curtains, drapes, and upholstery, and frequently add a vase of flowers for "a splash of color".

Color is important, psychologically and physiologically. In the booklet *COLOR DYNAMICS FOR THE HOME,* the Pittsburgh Plate Glass Company says: ". . . results (of the use of color in industry, educational institutions, office buildings, and homes) are due to the *energy* in color. Color, in the form of light, is part of the electro-magnetic spectrum . . . Variations in the number of impacts upon the eye affects muscular, mental, and nervous activity. For example, tests show that under ordinary light muscular activity is twenty-three empirical units. It advances slightly under blue light. Green light increases it a little more. Yellow light raises it to thirty units. Subject a person to a given color for as little as five minutes and his mental as well as his muscular activity changes."

It is obvious, then, that the color of your environment can have a profound effect on you and it therefore bears careful evaluation. In factories it has been found that absenteeism has decreased and morale, safety, even comfort, have been greatly increased by the judicious use of suitable colors.

The expert in the field of colors for home, office, school, factory, etc., is Faber Birren, who makes his living by prescribing color. "He prescribes it to government, to education, to the armed forces, to architecture, to industry and commerce" according to his book *COLOR PSYCHOLOGY AND COLOR THERAPY* (University Books, NY, 1961). One of the points he deals with is Visibility.

> "Visibility is one factor in color that may be readily measured. The ability to see clearly may be determined by experiment and test and requires neither feeling nor judgement . . . The eye sees best in white, yellowish, or yellowish-green light and worst in blue light. Thus sunglasses are gest when tinted either yellow or yellow-green. These colors may not only increase visibility and acuity by cutting down the excess brilliance of full sunlight, but they will screen out the disturbing influence of ultraviolet. In fact, on a sunny day yellow glasses may actually improve vision and help the eye to see more clearly into distance."

When speaking of environmental decoration he goes on to say:

"It is quite possible to set forthideal brightness specifications . . . Ceilings — almost without exception — should be white. This will be essential to the efficiency of indirect lighting systems. In direct systems, the white overhead will reduce contrasts between fixtures and their surroundings. Being 'neutral', white will also attract less psychological notice and hence prove non-distracting . . .

"For industrial purposes, soft, delicately grayish hues are best. They are lacking in aggression, less distracting, and they most effectively conceal dust and soiling. Ordinarily, primitive colors such as blue and yellow are tiresome. Where subtlety exists blueish-green, peach, etc.) a more comfortable environment will be found and one that will 'wear well' over prolonged periods. It is logical to use 'cool' colors such as green or blue where the working conditions expose the employee to relatively high temperatures. Conversely, 'warm' tones of ivory, cream, or peach are suitable to soften up a vaulty or chilly space and compensate for lack of natural light."

The colors we use in our personal appearance are as important as those in our surroundings. It is here, and in the home, that we can draw on chromology to boost our lives. In chapter three I showed how, through numerology, you can find the color(s) you are lacking. This can be expanded to show what color(s) you might need on a particular day, for it is not only Mondays that can be "blue". Many times we feel down on other days; days when there seems no special reason to feel that way. So let us examine Days.

Some books on color give a list showing the colors generally associated with each particular day of the week. I find these are not too accurate, for not *all* Mondays are the same, nor all Tuesdays, etc. . . . Each day is individual. To find the color associated with a particular day, then, you must return to numerology. Let's consider Friday, September 23, 1983, as an example

$$9.23.1983 = 9 + 2 + 3 + 1 + 9 + 8 + 3 = 35 = 8$$

This particular Friday is an 8 day and, from Chapter Three, we know that 8 is associated with the color Rose.

The following Friday is September 30.

$$9.30.1983 = 33 = 6$$

So that is a 6 day, or Indigo. You can see, then, that not all Fridays (or any other days of the week) are the same. Now how can you use this knowledge?

If the day's color is a "positive" one — a bright, warm, up-lifting one — then you probably won't want to alter it . . . just enjoy it. **But supposing it's at the other end of the** spectrum? Suppose, for example, that you see that this coming Tuesday is going to be a Blue day and Friday a Violet day? Fine — then you can be prepared for them and can counter any adverse/depressive effects by dressing accordingly. Dress in the *opposite* color, to counterbalance.

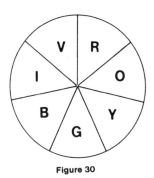

Figure 30

Opposite Blue are **Red and Orange.** On Tuesday use these colors liberally. Opposite Violet are Yellow and Green; use these colors liberally on Friday. You will find that the simple act of compensating for the less invigorating colors will keep you from getting depressed. *(See Fig. 30 for opposite colors).*

Conversely, of course, you may want to ward off an overabundance of energy. On a Red day, you may prefer to wear Blue and green, or Turquoise, and take it easy.

COLOR TREASURE MAPS

There is a magickal technique used to help in creating your own reality. It is the Treasure Map. Through the Treasure Map it is possible to manifest virtually anything that you desire. As a road map shows you how to get to your destination, so a Treasure Map helps you achieve your goals. It can be large or small; with or without elaborate pictures. Whatever its composition it is a means of keeping your intent on your goal; of keeping you always moving forward towards what you desire.

The very act of making a Treasure Map is a ritual for success. When making a magickal talisman (see chapter five), you put "power", or *mana*, into it by working on it personally; by directing your energies into it. So with the Treasure Map. And by incorporating color in its construction, you can really create an abundance of power, as you will see.

Many people feel that they are "not worthy" of the good

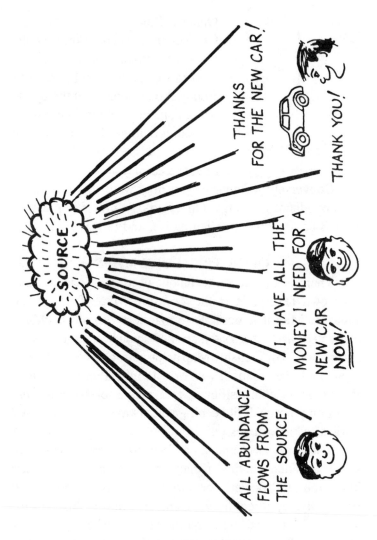

Figure 31

things in life. Or, perhaps through ingrained Christian or other religious training, feel that it is somehow "wrong" to have material possessions and/or wealth. Nothing could be further from the truth. We are all worthy of, and fully entitled to, the Universal Abundance. It is as much "right" for *you* to have what you want, as it is for anyone else to. The more you keep that thought in mind, the sooner you will achieve your desires. And the Color Treasure Map will make it happen.

It may seem unbelievable that simply by drawing and coloring pictures you can get what you want. It seems especially so when you can't draw too well and your efforts look like those of a nine-year-old! But don't despair . . . nine-year-olds generally have a *lot* of psychic energy.

Your map should be as simple as possible, with clear vivid pictures (we'll consider the pictureless one later). At the top center you need a picture of the "Source" of all things. This could be a God- or Goddess-like figure, or a symbol (such as the Infinity sign, the Chinese Yin-Yang, a Pentagram, Cross, or Star of David), or whatever, which to you personally is indicative of The Source.

Now show (draw) what you want, coming from this Source to you. Suppose, for example, you want enough money to buy a car. Then you might draw a Treasure Map something like that shown in *Figure 31.*

As you see, everything comes from the Source to *You.* I find it good to work in three steps — (i) *(on the left of the Treasure Map)* acknowledgement that everything comes from The Source. (ii) *(Center)* affirming that I have what I want, *and that I have it now.* (iii) *(Right of the Treasure Map)* giving thanks for receiving what I wanted.

The standard of drawing is not important. In fact I
would go so far as to say that the more basic it is, the better;
almost make it a caricature. In other words, don't try for
photographic realism. And — most important— *USE LOTS
OF BRIGHT COLORS.* If you are a blonde, for example,
draw yourself with bright yellow hair. Let The Source — be it
God, Goddess, Jesus, Ankh, Pentagram, or what/whomever
— be surrounded with *all* the colors.

Some people suggest that you find appropriate pictures
in magazines and cut them out, pasting them on to make your
Treasure Map. I think you'll find it much more effective to do
all the illustrating yourself. This way there are far more of
your energies going into the map, plus it is *exactly* what you
want, and not a compromise of any sort.

A pictureless Treasure Map *can* be made, if you really
feel that you can't draw at all. Instead of the pictures, then,
you simply write out, in plain, simple terms, exactly what it is
you want. Use as few words as possible and, again, use bright
colors for writing them. But I would again emphasize that
artistic skills are not important. It will be *far* better to draw —
however simply; however crudely — than to spell out.

What do you do with the map after it's made? Hang it
somewhere where you will see it frequently. Tape it to the
refrigerator door, to the side of a filing cabinet, to your
bedroom wall. Put it somewhere where you can keep looking
at it and keep going over, in your mind, all that it shows. Get
to where you can see it in your mind's eye when you are
riding the bus or train to work, when you are jogging, when
you are sleeping. Constantly seeing, and repeating, what the

Treasure Map shows will take you to your destination. It won't happen overnight, but it will happen.

Treasure Maps can be done for possessions, for jobs, love, health, business success, spiritual advancement . . . for anything. They are fun to do but, most importantly, they work. Remember— BASIC DRAWING and *BRIGHT COLORS*.

You can incorporate some of what you have learned about color correspondences, when making your map. For instance, if you are working for money, draw your map on green paper. Working for love? Use pink paper. Tranquility? Blue paper. and so on.

Suppose you want a number of things at one time? Well, there's no reason why you shouldn't put them all on one Treasure Map. A good idea, here, is to pattern it after the wheel of astrology. The astrological chart is divided up into twelve sections, known as Houses. These are equated with the signs of the Zodiac— the first house is Aries, the second Taurus, and so on *(Fig. 32)*.

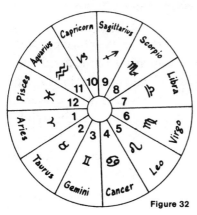

Additionally each House is equated with a particular area of life:

Figure 32

First House – Temperament; outward behavior; appearance; health.

Second House – Possessions; financial condition.

Third House – Brothers; sisters; communication; perceptive abilities; studies; mental aptitudes.

Fourth House – One of the parents; real estate; the home; domestic affairs; the beginning and the end of life.

Fifth House – Speculation; love affairs; pets; sexual urges; creative expressions.

Sixth House – Servants; sickness; hygiene; relationships between employer and employee; veterinarians.

Seventh House – Marriage partners; business partners; open (obvious) enemies; contracts.

Eighth House – Partner's money; attitude towards life and death; gifts; surgery.

Ninth House – Religious and philosophical outlooks; long journeys; foreigners and foreign countries; publishing; psychic development.

Tenth House – Standing in the community; reputation; social status; employment; the other parent (from the one in the Fourth House).

Eleventh House – Friends; social alliances; financial condition of employer; income from business when self-employed.

Twelfth House – Secret enemies; large animals; clandestine affairs; hospitalization; isolation; service to others.

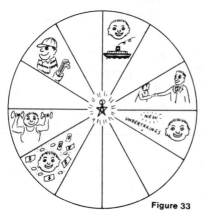

Figure 33

Suppose you want to improve your financial situation, take a trip to Europe, go into partnership to start a business with a friend, join the local country club, and do some body-building?

Financial situation would be covered in the Second House. Long journeys are in the Ninth. Partnerships are in the Seventh, and don't forget that the Fifth House also covers new undertakings. The Eleventh deals with social alliances, which would cover your country club aspirations. And the First House deals with your outward appearance. You could, then, do a Treasure Map something like that shown in *Figure 33.*

In addition to using bright colors in the whole rendition, consider also the colors associated with the astrological sun signs and, through them, with each of the houses: Aries – RED, Taurus – YELLOW, Gemini – VIOLET, Cancer – GREEN, Leo – ORANGE, Virgo – VIOLET, Libra – YELLOW, Scorpio – RED, Sagittarius – PURPLE, Capricorn – BLUE, Aquarius – INDIGO, Pisces – INDIGO. You could use those colors to do the backgrounds of those Houses you are using.

AFTERWORD

If nothing else, I hope that this book has sparked your interest in color and its many uses. As I said in the Introduction, "since the beginning of time, colors have been endowed with magick." I have here shown a few simple ways to use that magick, for better health, wealth, and happiness. It is a form of magick that anyone can use, without elaborate equipment, without special training, and especially without any danger. It is *practical.*

Do the color meditations. Try the divination. Experiment with the magick. Make Treasure Maps and do healing. And try your own experiments and variations. The beneficial uses of magick are almost infinite. I have included what I believe to be one of the most comprehensive bibliographies available on the subject. Use it. Read every book you can and open for yourself the Rainbow of Existence . . . a life filled with color.

Raymond Buckland
Charlottesville, Virginia

BIBLIOGRAPHY

ABBOTT, Arthur G. - *The Mysteries of Color*. Aries Press, IL 1977

AMBER, Reuben B. - *Color Therapy*. Aurora Press, NY 1983

ANDERSON, Mary - *Color Healing*. Weiser, NY 1975

BABBITT, Edwin D. - *The Principles of Light and Color*. Babbitt, NY 1878

BASFORD, L & J - *The Rays of Light*. Sampson Low, Marston, London 1966

BHATTACHARYYA, B. - *VIBGYOR, The Science of Cosmic Ray Therapy*. Good Companions, India 1957

BIRREN, Faber - *Color Psychology and Color Therapy*. University Books, NY 1961

BIRREN, Faber - *New Horizons in Color*. Reinhold, NY 1955

BOOS-HAMBURGER, H. - *The Creative Power of Color*. New Knowledge Books, Sussex, England

BRAGG, William - *The Universe of Light*. Dover, NY 1959

BRUNLER, Oscar - *Rays and Radiation Phenomena*. DeVorss, CA 1948

BUTLER, W.E. - *How To Read the Aura*. Weiser, NY 1971

CAYCE, Edgar - *Gems and Stones*. A.R.E. Press, VA 1976

CAYCE, Edgar - *Auras*. A.R.E. Press, VA 1973

CHEVREUL, M.E. - *The Principles Of Harmony and Contrast Of Colors*. Bell & Dalby, London 1870

CHRAPOWICKI, Maryla de - *The Power of Sound and Health, Strength and Union*. Med Soc. For the Study of Radiesthesia, London

CHRAPOWICKI, Maryla de - *SpectroBiology*. Health Research, CA 1938

CLARK, Linda - *The Ancient Art of Color Therapy*. Devin-Adair, CT 1975

CLARK, L & MARTINE, Y - *Health, Youth and Beauty Through Color Breathing*. Celestial Arts, CA 1976

CLEMENT, Mark - *Waves That Heal*. Health Research, CA

COOPER-HUNT, C.L. - *Radiesthetic Analysis*. Health Research, CA 1969

COPEN, Bruce - *Heal Yourself With Color*. Academic Publications Sussex, England 1974

COPEN Bruce – *Character Analysis With Color.* Academic Publications, Sussex, England 1976

CORTE, L.P. – *Sound and Vibration Measurement.* Med. Soc. For the Study of Radiesthesia, London

DON, Frank – *Color Your World.* Warner Destiny Books, NY 1977

EVANS, Ralph, M. – *An Introduction to Color.* Wiley, NY 1948

FERNIE, W.T. – *Precious Stones (Curative).* Wright, Bristol, England 1907

FIELDING, William, J. – *The Marvels and Oddities Of Sunlight.* Haldeman-Julius, KS

FINCH, W.J. & E. – *Photo-Chromotherapy.* Esoteric Publications, AZ 1972

GHADIALI, Dinshah P. – *Spectro-Chrome Metry Encyclopaedia.* Vols. 1, 2, 3, Spectro-Chrome Institute, NJ 1939

GHADIALI, Dinshah P. – *Family Health Protector.* Spectro-Chrome Institute, NJ 1943

GOETHE, Johann W. von – *Theory Of Colours.* M.I.T. Press, MA 1970

GRAVES, Maitland – *The Art of Color and Design.* McGraw-Hill, NY 1941

GRAVES, Maitland – *Color Fundamentals.* McGraw-Hill, NY 1952

HANOKA, N.S. – *The Advantages Of Healing By Visible Spectrum Therapy.* Bharti Association, India 1957

HEBING, J. – *Letters On the Theory Of Colour.* New Knowledge Books, Sussex, England

HELINE, Corinne – *Healing and Regeneration Through Color.* New Age Press, CA 1976

HELINE, Corinne – *Healing and Regeneration Through Music.* New Age Press, CA 1978

HETHERINGTON, Rex D. – *Color — Its Power, Action and Therapeutic Value.* Boston, MA

HOFFMAN, Edith – *Huna, A Beginner's Guide.* Para Research, MA 1976

HOWAT, R.D. – *Elements Of Chromotherapy.* Actinic, London, 1938

HUNT, Roland T. – *Complete Color Prescription.* DeVorss, CA 1962

HUNT, Roland T. – *The Seven Keys To Color Healing.* C.W. Daniel, London 1971

HUNT, Roland T. – *The Eighth Key To Color.* Fowler, London 1965

HUNT, Roland T. – *Fragrant and Radiant Healing Symphony.* London 1937

JACKSON, Carole – *Color Me Beautiful.* Ballantine Books, NY 1980

JACOBSON, Egbert – *Basic Colour.* Theobald, IL 1948

JENSEN, Dr. E.T. – *Some Steps In Radiesthetic Technique.* Med. Soc. For the Study Of Radiesthesia, London, England

KARGERE, Audrey – *Color and Personality.* Wehman, NY

KATZ, David – *The World of Color.* Kegan Paul, London 1935

KELLY, K.L. & JUDD, D.B. – *Color — Universal Language and Dictionary Of Names.* U.S. Dept. of Commerce 1976

KILNER, Walter J. – *The Aura.* Weiser, NY 1973

KLEIN, Adrian B. – *Colour-Music.* Lockwood, London 1930

LADD-FRANKLIN, Christine – *Colour and Colour Theories.* Von Nostrand, NY 1929

LEADBETTER, C.W. – *Man Visible and Invisible.* Theosophical Soc., London 1971

LEWIS, Roger – *Color and the Edgar Cayce Readings.* A.R.E. Press, VA 1973

LUCKIESH, Matthew – *Color and Its Implications.* Van Nostrand, NY 1921

LUCKEISH, Matthew – *Ultra Violet Radiation.* Van Nostrand, NY 1922

LUCKEISH, Matthew – *Color and Colors.* Van Nostrand, NY 1938

LUCKEISH, M. & PACINI, A.J. – *Light and Health.* Williams & Williams, MD 1926

MAERZ, A. & PAUL, M.P. – *A Dictionary Of Color.* McGraw-Hill, NY 1930

MAYER, Gladys – *Colour and Healing.* New Knowledge Books Sussex, England 1974

MAYER, Gladys – *The Mystery-Wisdom Of Colour.* New Knowledge Books, Sussex, England

MAYER, Gladys – *Colour and the Human Soul.* New Knowledge Books, Sussex, England

MERMET, Abbé – *Principles and Practices of Radiesthesia.* Watkins, London 1975

OSTWALD, Wilhelm – *Colour Science.* Winsor & Newton, London 1931

OTT, John N. - *Health and Light.* Pocket Books, NY 1976

OUSELEY, S.G.J. - *Color Meditations.* Fowler, Essex, England 1949

OUSELEY, S.G.J. - *The Power of the Rays.* Fowler, Essex, England 1951

PANCOAST, S - *Blue and Red Light.* Stoddart, PA 1877

PITTSBURGH PLATE GLASS COMPANY - *Color Dynamics For the Home.* P.P.G.Co, FL

RAMADAHN - *Colour and Healing For the New Age.* Roberts, London

RICHARDS, Dr. Guyon - *Medical Dowsing.* Med. Soc. For the Study of Radiesthesia, London

SANDBACK, John - *The Mysteries Of Color.* Aries Press, IL 1977

SANDER, C.G. - *Colour In Health and Disease.* Daniel, London 1926

SANDER, C.G. - *The Seven Keys Of Colour Healing.* Daniel, London 1928

SARGENT, Walter - *The Enjoyment and Use Of Color.* Scribner's, NY 1923

SCOTT, Ian (tr. & Ed.) - *The Lüscher Color Test of Dr. Max Lüscher.* Random House, NY 1969

STEINER, Rudolf - *Colour.* New Knowledge Books, Sussex, England

STEVENS, Ernest J. - *Lights, Colors, Tones and Nature's Finer Forces.* Stevens, CA 1923

STURZAKER, D. & J. - *Colour and the Kabbalah.* Weiser, NY 1975

TARPEY, Kingsley - *Healing By Radiesthesia.* Med. Soc. For the Study Of Radiesthesia, London, England

THEDICK, Eleanore - *The Bridge Of Color.* Christ Ministry Foundation, CA

THRONTON, Dr. R.G. - *Rays, Radiations and the Psychophysical Organism.* Medical Society For the Study of Radiesthesia, London, England

TIME-LIFE BOOKS - *Color.* NY 1970

TOMLINSON, Dr. H. - *The Use Of the Pendulum In Medicine.* Med. Soc. for the Study of Radiesthesia, London, England

TURNER, Albert E. - *A Study of Color.* Pts. I, II, III, *The Searchlight,* v.15 No. 8 (Aug. 1963), v.15 No. 11 (Nov. 1963), v.16 No. 2 (Feb. 1964) A.R.E.Press, VA

VARIOUS AUTHORS – Color Healing. Health Research, CA 1956

VERHOVEN, Marion - Music Therapy. from Chinese Magazine Brea, CA Spring 1952

WETHERED, Vernon D. The Practice of Medical Radiesthesia. C.W. Daniel, London 1977

WILLEY, Raymond C. - Modern Dowsing. Esoteric Publications, AZ 1976

WILSON, M. - What Is Color?. New Knowledge Books, Sussex, England

WRIGHT, W.D. - The Measurement Of Colour. Hilger, London 1944

Journals

RADIONIC QUARTERLY - Journal of the Radionic Association, Guildford, Surrey, England

RADIESTHESIA - Journal of the Medical Society For the Study Of Radiesthesia, London, England

INDEX

STAY IN TOUCH

On the following pages you will find some related books. Your book dealer stocks most of these and will stock new titles in the Llewellyn series as they become available. We urge your patronage.

To obtain our full catalog, to keep informed about new titles as they are released and to benefit from informative articles and helpful news, you are invited to write for our bimonthly news magazine/catalog, *Llewellyn's New Worlds of Mind and Spirit*. A sample copy is free, and it will continue coming to you at no cost as long as you are an active mail customer. Or you may subscribe for just $10.00 in the U.S.A. and Canada ($20.00 overseas, first class mail). Many bookstores also have *New Worlds* available to their customers. Ask for it.

Llewellyn's New Worlds of Mind and Spirit
P.O. Box 64383-047, St. Paul, MN 55164-0383, U.S.A.
* * *

TO ORDER BOOKS AND TAPES

If your book dealer does not have the books described, you may order them directly from the publisher by sending full price in U.S. funds, plus $3.00 for postage and handling for orders *under* $10.00; $4.00 for orders *over* $10.00. There are no postage and handling charges for orders over $50.00. Postage and handling rates are subject to change. We ship UPS whenever possible. Delivery guaranteed. Provide your street address as UPS does not deliver to P.O. Boxes. UPS to Canada requires a $50.00 minimum order. Allow 4-6 weeks for delivery. Orders outside the U.S.A. and Canada: Airmail—add retail price of book; add $5.00 for each non-book item (tapes, etc.); add $1.00 per item for surface mail.

FOR GROUP STUDY AND PURCHASE

Because there is a great deal of interest in group discussion and study of the subject matter of this book, we offer a special quantity price to group leaders or agents. Our Special Quantity Price for a minimum order of five copies of *Practical Color Magick* is $20.85 cash-with-order. This price includes postage and handling within the United States. Minnesota residents must add 6.5% sales tax. For additional quantities, please order in multiples of five. For Canadian and foreign orders, add postage and handling charges as above. Credit card (VISA, MasterCard, American Express) orders are accepted. Charge card orders only may be phoned in free within the U.S.A. or Canada by dialing 1-800-THE-MOON. For customer service, call 1-612-291-1970. Mail orders to:

LLEWELLYN PUBLICATIONS
P.O. Box 64383-047, St. Paul, MN 55164-0383, U.S.A.

Prices subject to change without notice.

MAGICAL HERBALISM: The Secret Craft of the Wise
by Scott Cunningham

In Magical Herbalism, certain plants are prized for the special range of energies—the vibrations, or powers—they possess. Magical Herbalism unites the powers of plants and man to produce, and direct, change in accord with human will and desire.

This is the Magic of amulets and charms, sachets and herbal pillows, incenses and scented oils, simples and infusions and anointments. It's Magic as old as our knowledge of plants, an art that anyone can learn and practice, and once again enjoy as we look to the Earth to rediscover our roots and make inner connections with the world of Nature.

This is Magic that is beautiful and natural—a Craft of Hand and Mind merged with the Power and Glory of Nature: a special kind that does not use the medicinal powers of herbs, but rather the subtle vibrations and scents that touch the psychic centers and stir the astral field in which we live to work at the causal level behind the material world.

This is the Magic of Enchantment . . . of word and gesture to shape the images of mind and channel the energies of the herbs. It is a Magic for *everyone*—for the herbs are easily and readily obtained, the tools are familiar or easily made, and the technology that of home and garden. This book includes step-by-step guidance to the preparation of herbs and to their compounding in incense and oils, sachets and amulets, simples and infusions, with simple rituals and spells for every purpose.

0-87542-120-2, 256 pgs., 5 1/4 x 8, illus., softcover   **$7.95**

PRACTICAL CANDLEBURNING RITUALS
by Raymond Buckland, Ph.D.

Another book in Llewellyn's Practical Magick series. Magick is a way in which to apply the full range of your hidden psychic powers to the problems we all face in daily life. We know that normally we use only 5% of our total powers—Magick taps powers from deep inside our psyche where we are in contact with the Universe's limitless resources.

Magick need not be complex—it can be as simple as using a few candles to focus your mind, a simple ritual to give direction to your desire, a few words to give expression to your wish.

This book shows you how easy it can be. Here is Magick for fun, Magick as a Craft, Magick for Success. Love, Luck, Money, Marriage, Healing; Magick to stop slander, to learn truth, to heal an unhappy marriage, to overcome a bad habit, to break up a love affair, etc.

Magick—with nothing fancier than ordinary candles, and the 28 rituals in this book (given in both Christian and Old Religion versions)—can transform your life. Illustrated.

0–87542-048-6, 189 pgs., 5 1/4 x 8, softcover   **$6.95**

THE BUCKLAND GYPSY FORTUNETELLING DECK
by Ray Buckland

The Buckland Gypsy Fortunetelling Deck is a deck of 74 cards consisting of 22 Major Arcana and 52 Minor Arcana. They are very different from the Tarot, and are a fascinating and effective tool for divination. Created by Ray Buckland, himself a Gypsy, they are authentic and realistic.

Over the past 200 years some Romani families have designed their own Major Arcana to be used with a regular deck. These new cards often bore no resemblance to the Major Arcana of the Tarot, and even varied greatly from one Gypsy family to the next.

One such Romani deck is that of the Buckland family of Gypsies, presented here for the first time ever. *The Buckland Gypsy Fortunetelling Deck* is complete. Included with the deck is a 36-page instruction book that includes all necessary information needed to use the cards. The booklet contains an introduction to the deck, the meaning of each card, the names of each Major Arcana card, and includes several original divinatory spreads.

0-87542-052-4   **$12.95**

SECRETS OF GYPSY FORTUNETELLING
by Ray Buckland

This book unveils the Romani secrets of fortune-telling, explaining in detail the many different methods used by these nomads. For generations they have survived on their skills as seers. Their accuracy is legendary. They are a people who seem to be born with "the sight" . . . the ability to look into the past, present and future using only the simplest of tools to aid them. Here you will learn to read palms, to interpret the symbols in a teacup, to read cards . . . both the Tarot and regular playing cards. Here are revealed the secrets of interpreting the actions of animals, of reading the weather, of recognizing birthmarks and the shape of hands. Impress your friends with your knowledge of many of these lesser Mysteries; uncommon forms of fortune-telling known only to a few.

The methods of divination presented in this book are all practical methods—no expensive or hard-to-get items are necessary. The Gypsies are accomplished at using natural objects and everyday items to serve them in their endeavors. Sticks and stones, knives and needles, cards and dice . . . some are found along the roadside, or in the woods, others are easily obtainable at little expense from the five-and-dime, the convenience store, or the traveling peddler. Using these non-complex objects, and following the traditional Gypsy ways shown, you can become a seer and improve the quality of your own life and of these lives around you.

0-87542-051-6, mass market format, 220 pgs., illus.   **$3.95**

BUCKLAND'S COMPLETE GYPSY FORTUNE TELLER
by Raymond Buckland

Buckland's Complete Gypsy Fortune Teller is a new kit from Llewellyn giving you everything you need to perform divination in the Gypsy tradition. Included is the book *Secrets of Gypsy Fortunetelling*, in which the secrets of divination with palms, tea leaves, cards, dice and other methods are revealed.

You can use the insights gained from the book to perform powerful divination with *The Buckland Gypsy Fortunetelling Deck*. This 74-card deck has a distinctive Romani (Gypsy) Major Arcana, and a Minor Arcana composed of a regular poker deck. A handy 16" by 24", four-color layout sheet is included, making the deck instantly and easily usable. Each side illustrates a different layout—the Seven Star layout and the Romani Star layout. With this you can discover future events, hopes, fears, strengths and much more.

All of these attractive and useful items are packaged neatly into a convenient box under 9 1/2" tall and about the width of a thick book. A one-of-a-kind kit that makes a surprising and intriguing gift, *Buckland's Complete Fortune Teller* reflects the nuances of Gypsy culture while bringing a potential for improvement in *anybody's* life.

0-87542-055-9, book, 74-card deck, layout sheet $19.95

THE COMPLETE BOOK OF INCENSE, OILS AND BREWS
by Scott Cunningham

For centuries the composition of incenses, the blending of oils, and the mixing of herbs have been used by people to create positive changes in their lives. With this book, the curtains of secrecy have been drawn back, providing you with practical, easy-to-understand information that will allow you to practice these methods of magical cookery.

Scott Cunningham, world-famous expert on magical herbalism, first published *The Magic of Incense, Oils and Brews* in 1986. *The Complete Book of Incense, Oils and Brews* is a revised and expanded version of that book. Scott took readers' suggestions from the first edition and added more than 100 new formulas. Every page has been clarified and rewirtten, and new chapters have been added.

There is no special, costly equipment to buy, and ingredients are usually easy to find. The book includes detailed information on a wide variety of herbs, sources for purchasing ingredients, substitutions for hard-to-find herbs, a glossary, and a chapter on creating your own magical recipes.

0-87542-128-8, 288 pgs., 5 1/4 x 8, illus., softcover $12.95

EARTH POWER: TECHNIQUES OF NATURAL MAGIC
by Scott Cunningham

Magick is the art of working with the forces of Nature to bring about necessary, and desired, changes. The forces of Nature—expressed through Earth, Air, Fire and Water—are our "spiritual ancestors" who paved the way for our emergence from the pre-historic seas of creation. Attuning to, and working with these energies in magick not only lends you the power to affect changes in your life, it also allows you to sense your own place in the larger scheme of Nature. Using the "Old Ways" enables you to live a better life, and to deepen your understanding of the world about you. The tools and powers of magick are around you, waiting to be grasped and utilized. This book gives you the means to put Magick into your life, shows you how to make and use the tools, and gives you spells for every purpose.

0-87542-121-0, 176 pgs., 5¼ x 8, illus., softcover **$6.95**

CRYSTAL POWER
by Michael G. Smith

This is an amazing book, for what it claims to present—with complete instructions and diagrams so that YOU can work them yourself—is the master technology of ancient Atlantis: psionic (mind-controlled and life-energized machines) devices made from common quartz crystals!

Learn to easily construct an "Atlantean" Power Rod that can be used for healing or a weapon; or a Crystal Headband stimulating psychic powers; or a Time and Space Communications Generator; operated purely by your mind.

These crystal devices seem to work only with the disciplined mind power of a human operator, yet their very construction seems to start a process of growth and development, a new evolutionary step in the human psyche that bridges mind and matter.

Does this "re-discovery" mean that we are living, now, in the New Atlantis? Have these Power Tools been re-invented to meet the needs of this prophetic time? Are Psionic Machines the culminating Power To the People to free us from economic dependence on fossil fuels and smoke-stack industry?

This book answers "yes" to all these questions, and asks you to simply build these devices and put them to work to help bring it all about.

0-87542-725-1, 288 pgs., illus., 5¼ x 8, softcover **$9.95**

THE LLEWELLYN PRACTICAL GUIDE TO
ASTRAL PROJECTION
The Out-of-Body Experience
by Denning & Phillips

Yes, your consciousness can be sent forth, out of the body, with full awareness and return with full memory. You can travel through time and space, converse with nonphysical entities, obtain knowledge by nonmaterial means, and experience higher dimensions.

Is there life after death? Are we forever shackled by time and space? The ability to go forth by means of the Astral Body, or Body of Light, gives the personal assurance of consciousness (and life) beyond the limitations of the physical body. No other answer to these ageless questions is as meaningful as experienced reality. The reader is led through the essential stages for the inner growth and development that will culminate in fully conscious projection and return. Not only are the requisite practices set forth in step-by-step procedures, augmented with photographs and visualization aids, but the vital reasons for undertaking them are clearly explained.

Guidance is also given to the Astral World what to expect, what can be done—including the ecstatic experience of Astral Sex between two people who project together into this higher world where true union is consummated free of the barriers of physical bodies.
0-87542-181-4, 266 pgs., 5 ¼ x 8, illus., softcover **$8.95**

THE LLEWELLYN DEEP MIND TAPE
FOR ASTRAL PROJECTION
by Denning & Phillips

The authors of Llewellyn's Practical Guide to Astral Projection are adepts fully experienced in all levels of psychic development and training, and have designed this 90-minute cassette tape to guide you through full relaxation and all the preparations for projection, and then—with the added dimension of the author's personally produced electronic synthesizer patterns of sound and music—they program the Deep Mind through the stages of awakening, and projection of, the astral Body of Light. And then the programming guides your safe return to normal consciousness with memory— enabling you to bridge the worlds of Body, Mind and Spirit. The Deep Mind Tape is a powerful new technique combining guided Mind Programming with specially created sound and music to evoke deep level response in the psyche and its psychic centers for controlled development, and induction of the Out-of-Body Experience.
0-87542-168-7, 90 minute cassette tape **$9.95**

THE LLEWELLYN PRACTICAL GUIDE TO
CREATIVE VISUALIZATION
For the Fulfillment of Your Desires
by Denning & Phillips

All things you will ever want must have their start in your mind. The average person uses very little of the full creative power that is his, potentially. It's like the power locked in the atom—it's all there, but you have to learn to release it and apply it constructively. Some people apply this innate power without actually knowing what they are doing, and achieve great success and happiness; most people, however, use this same power, again unknowingly, incorrectly, and experience bad luck, failure, or at best an unfulfilled life.

This book changes that. Through an easy series of step-by-step, progressive exercises, your mind is applied to bring desire into realization! Wealth, power, success, happiness even psychic powers ... even what we call magickal power and spiritual attainment ... all can be yours. You can easily develop this completely natural power, and correctly apply it, for your immediate and practical benefit. Illustrated with unique, "puts-you-into-the-picture" visualization aids.

0-87542-183-0, 294 pgs., 5-¼ x 8, illus., softcover $8.95

THE LLEWELLYN PRACTICAL GUIDE TO
THE DEVELOPMENT OF PSYCHIC POWERS
by Denning & Phillips

You may not realize it, but you already have the ability to use ESP, Astral Vision and Clairvoyance, Divination, Dowsing, Prophecy, and Communication with Spirits. Written by two of the most knowledgeable experts in the world of psychic development, this book is a complete course—teaching you, step-by-step, how to develop these powers that actually have been yours since birth. Using the techniques, you will soon be able to move objects at a distance, see into the future, know the thoughts and feelings of another person, find lost objects and locate water using your no-longer latent talents.

Psychic powers are a natural ability like any other talent. You'll learn to play with these new skills, working with groups of friends to accomplish things you never would have believed possible before reading this book. The text shows how to make the equipment you can use, the exercises you can do—many of them at any time, anywhere—and how to use your abilities to change your life and the lives of those close to you. Many of the exercises are presented in forms that can be adapted as games for pleasure and fun, as well as development.

0-87542-191-1, 272 pgs., 5 ¼ x 8, illus., softcover $8.95

THE LLEWELLYN PRACTICAL GUIDE TO
PSYCHIC SELF-DEFENSE AND WELL-BEING
by Denning & Phillips

Psychic well-being and psychic self-defense are two sides of the same coin, just as are physical health and resistance to disease. Each person (and every living thing) is surrounded by an electromagnetic force field, or AURA, that can provide the means to psychic self-defense and to dynamic well-being. This book explores the world of very real "psychic warfare" of which we are all victims.

Every person in our modern world is subjected to psychic stress and psychological bombardment: advertising promotions that play upon primitive emotions, political and religious appeals that work on feelings of insecurity and guilt, noise, threats of violence and war, news of crime and disaster, etc.

This book shows the nature of genuine psychic attacks—ranging from actual acts of black magic to bitter jealousy and hate—and the reality of psychic stress, the structure of the psyche and its interrelationship with the physical body. It shows how each person must develop his weakened aura into a powerful defense-shield, thereby gaining both physical protection and energetic well-being that can extend to protection from physical violence, accidents … even ill health.

0-87542-190-3, 306 pgs., 5 ¼ x 8, illus., softcover $8.95

THE LLEWELLYN PRACTICAL GUIDE TO
THE MAGICK OF THE TAROT
by Denning & Phillips

"To gain understanding, and control, of Your Life"—Can anything be more important? To gain insight into the circumstances of your life–the inner causes, the karmic needs—and then to have the power to change your life in order to fulfill your real desires and True Will: that's what the techniques taught in this book can do.

Discover the Shadows cast ahead by Coming Events. Yes, this is possible, because it is your DEEP MIND—that part of your psyche, normally beyond your conscious awareness, which is in touch with the World Soul and with your own Higher (and Divine) Self—that perceives the astral shadows of coming events and can communicate them to you through the symbols and images of the ancient and mysterious Tarot Cards. Your Deep Mind has the power to shape those astral shadows—images that are causal to material events—when you learn to communicate your own desires and goals using the Tarot.

0–87542–198–9, 252 pgs., 5¼ x 8, illus., softcover $7.95

HOW TO HEAL WITH COLOR
by Ted Andrews

Now, for perhaps the first time, color therapy is placed within the grasp of the average individual. Anyone can learn to facilitate and accelerate the healing process on all levels with the simple color therapies in *How to Heal with Color*.

Color serves as a vibrational remedy that interacts with the human energy system to stabilize physical, emotional, mental and spiritual conditions. When there is balance, we can more effectively rid ourselves of toxins, negativities and patterns that hinder our life processes.

This book provides color application guidelines that are beneficial for over 50 physical conditions and a wide variety of emotional and mental conditions. Receive simple and tangible instructions for performing "muscle testing" on yourself and others to find the most beneficial colors. Learn how to apply color therapy through touch, projection, breathing, cloth, water and candles. Learn how to use the little known but powerful color-healing system of the mystical Qabala to balance and open the psychic centers. Plus, discover simple techniques for performing long distance healings on others.

0-87542-005-2, 240 pgs., mass market, illus.   **$3.95**

CRYSTAL HEALING
The Next Step
by Phyllis Galde

Discover the further secrets of quartz crystal! Now modern research and use have shown that crystals have even more healing and therapeutic properties than have been realized. Learn why polished, smoothed crystal is better to use to heighten your intuition, improve creativity and for healing.

Learn to use crystals for reprogramming your subconscious to eliminate problems and negative attitudes that prevent success. Here are techniques that people have successfully used, not just theories. This book reveals newly discovered abilities of crystal now accessible to all, and is a sensible approach to crystal use. *Crystal Healing* will be your guide to improve the quality of your life and expand your consciousness.

0-87542-246-2, 224 pgs., mass market, illus.   **$3.95**

A GARDEN OF POMEGRANATES
by Israel Regardie
What is the Tree of Life? It's the ground plan of the Qabalistic system—a set of symbols used since ancient times to study the Universe. The Tree of Life is a geometrical arrangement of ten sephiroth, or spheres, each of which is associated with a different archetypal idea, and 22 paths which connect the spheres.

This system of primal correspondences has been found the most efficient plan ever devised to classify and organize the characteristics of the self. Israel Regardie has written one of the best and most lucid introductions to the Qabalah.

A Garden of Pomegranates combines Regardie's own studies with his notes on the works of Aleister Crowley, A.E. Waite, Eliphas Levi and D.H. Lawrence. No longer is the wisdom of the Qabalah to be held *secret!* The needs of today place the burden of growth upon each and every person— each has to undertake the Path as his or her own responsibility, but every help is given in the most ancient and yet most modern teaching here known to humankind.

0-87542-690-5, 176 pgs., softcover **$6.95**

THE MIDDLE PILLAR
by Israel Regardie
Between the two outer pillars of the Qabalistic Tree of Life, the extremes of Mercy and Severity, stands THE MIDDLE PILLAR, signifying one who has achieved equilibrium in his or her own self.

Integration of the human personality is vital to the continuance of creative life. Without it, man lives as an outsider to his own true self. By combining Magic and Psychology in the Middle Pillar Ritual/Exercise (a magical meditation technique), we bring into balance the opposing elements of the psyche while yet holding within their essence and allowing full expression of man's entire being.

In this book, and with this practice, you will learn to: understand the psyche through its correspondences on the Tree of Life; expand self-awareness, thereby intensifying the inner growth process; activate creative and intuitive potentials; understand the individual thought patterns which control every facet of personal behavior; regain the sense of balance and peace of mind—the equilibrium that everyone needs for physical and psychic health.

0-87542-658-1, 176 pgs., softcover **$6.95**

BUCKLAND'S COMPLETE BOOK OF WITCHCRAFT
by Raymond Buckland

Here is the most complete resource to the study and practice of modern, non-denominational Wicca. This is a lavishly illustrated, self-study course for the solitary or group. Included are rituals; exercises for developing psychic talents; information on all major "sects" of the Craft; sections on tools, beliefs, dreams, meditations, divination, herbal lore, healing, ritual clothing and much, much more. This book unites theory and practice into a comprehensive course designed to help you develop into a practicing Witch, one of the "Wise Ones."

Never before has so much information on the Craft of the Wise been collected in one place. Traditionally, there are three degrees of advancement in most Wiccan traditions. When you have completed studying this book, you will be the equivalent of a Third-Degree Witch. Even those who have practiced Wicca for years find useful information in this book, and many covens are using this for their textbook. If you want to become a Witch, or if you merely want to find out what Witchcraft is really about, you will find no better book than this.

0-87542-050-8, 272 pgs., 8 ½ x 11, illus., softcover $14.95

THE PRISTINE YI KING
Pure Wisdom of Ancient China
by Louis Culling

In this book you will discover the history of the Yi King (I Ching). You may be surprised to find out that it has gone through five evolutions and much has been added to its original simplicity. You will also discover how the Yi King was originally used and how you can easily use it today to effect positive change in your life. This book marks the first time that the Yi King has appeared in pristine form. It gives the true order of the hexagrams, thereby letting you memorize their order and meanings; it also defines the special relationship between chess and divination.

The Yi King is a fantastic system of philosophy and divination. Based on the polarity of opposites, it takes into account the fact that we are living in a sea of ever-fluctuating energy currents. Our universe is the manifestation of these forces seeking equilibrium, and these forces are expressed in the 64 Hexagrams of the Logical Square. This book explains the hexagrams in detail. It will undoubtedly be very popular with all seeking powerful divination or a means of inner growth.

0-87542-107-5, 224 pgs., 5 ¼ x 8, softcover $7.95

THE LLEWELLYN ANNUALS

Llewellyn's MOON SIGN BOOK: Approximately 500 pages of valuable information on gardening, fishing, weather, stock market forecasts, personal horoscopes, good planting dates, and general instructions for finding the best date to do just about anything! Articles by prominent forecasters and writers in the fields of gardening, astrology, politics, economics and cycles. Published annually since 1906, this fun, informative and has been a great help to millions in their daily planning. **State year $4.99**

Llewellyn's SUN SIGN BOOK: Your personal horoscope for the entire year! All 12 signs are included in one handy book. Also included are forecasts, special feature articles, and an action guide for each sign. Monthly horoscopes are written by Gloria Star, author of *Optimum Child*, for your personal sun sign and there are articles on a variety of subjects written by well-known astrologers from around the country. Much more than just a horoscope guide! Entertaining and fun the year around. **State year $4.99**

Llewellyn's DAILY PLANETARY GUIDE: Includes all of the major daily aspects plus their exact times in Eastern and Pacific time zones, lunar phases, signs and voids plus their times, planetary motion, a monthly ephemeris, sunrise and sunset tables, special articles on the planets, signs, aspects, a business guide, planetary hours, rulerships, and much more. Large 5-1/4 x 8 format for more writing space, spiral bound to lie flat, address and phone listings, time-zone conversion chart and blank horoscope chart. **State year $7.95**

Llewellyn's ASTROLOGICAL CALENDAR: Large wall calendar of 48 pages. Beautiful full-color cover and full-color paintings inside. Includes special feature articles by famous astrologers, and complete introductory information on astrology. It also contains a lunar gardening guide, celestial phenomena, a blank horoscope chart, and monthly date pages which include aspects, Moon phases, signs and voids, planetary motion, an ephemeris, personal forecasts, lucky dates, planting and fishing dates, and more. 10 x 13 size. **State year $10.00**

Llewellyn's MAGICAL ALMANAC: This beautifully illustrated almanac explores traditional earth religions and folklore while focusing on magical myths. Each month is summarized in a two-page format with information that includes the phases of the moon, festivals and rites for the month, as well as detailed magical advice. This is an indispensable guide is for anyone who is interested in planning rituals, spells and other magical advice. It features writing by some of the most prominent authors in the field. **State year $6.95**

MAGICAL AROMATHERAPY
The Power of Scent
by Scott Cunningham

Scent magic has a rich, colorful history. Today, in the shadow of the next century, there is much we can learn from the simple plants that grace our planet. Most have been used for countless centuries. The energies still vibrate within their aromas.

Scott Cunningham has now combined the current knowledge of the physiological and psychological effects of natural fragrances with the ancient art of magical perfumery. In writing this book, he drew on extensive experimentation and observation, research into 4,000 years of written records, and the wisdom of respected aromatherapy practitioners. *Magical Aromatherapy* contains a wealth of practical tables of aromas of the seasons, days of the week, the planets, and zodiac; use of essential oils with crystals; synthetic and genuine oils and hazardous essential oils. It also contains a handy appendix of aromatherapy organizations and distributors of essential oils and dried plant products.

0-87542-129-6, 224 pgs., mass market, illus. **$3.95**

WHEEL OF THE YEAR
Living the Magical Life
by Pauline Campanelli, illus. by Dan Campanelli

If you feel elated by the celebrations of the Sabbats and hunger for that feeling during the long weeks between Sabbats, *Wheel of the Year* can help you put the joy and fulfillment of magic into your everyday life. This book shows you how to celebrate the lesser changes in Nature. The wealth of seasonal rituals and charms are all easily performed with materials readily available and are simple and concise enough that the practitioner can easily adapt them to work within the framework of his or her own Pagan tradition.

Learn to perform fire magic in November, the secret Pagan symbolism of Christmas tree ornaments, the best time to visit a fairy forest or sacred spring and what to do when you get there. Learn the charms and rituals and the making of magical tools that coincide with the nesting season of migratory birds. Whether you are a newcomer to the Craft or have found your way back many years ago, *Wheel of the Year* will be an invaluable reference book in your practical magic library. It is filled with magic and ritual for everyday life and will enhance any system of Pagan Ritual.

0-87542-091-5, 176 pgs., 7 x 10, illus., softcover **$9.95**

DOORS TO OTHER WORLDS
A Practical Guide to Communicating with Spirits
by Raymond Buckland

There has been a revival of spiritualism in recent years, with more and more people attempting to communicate with disembodied spirits via talking boards, séances, and all forms of mediumship (e.g., allowing another spirit to make use of your vocal chords, hand muscles, etc., while you remain in control of your body). The movement, which began in 1848 with the Fox sisters of New York, has attracted the likes of Abraham Lincoln and Queen Victoria, and even blossomed into a full-scale religion with regular services of hymns, prayers, Bible-reading and sermons along with spirit communication.

Doors to Other Worlds is for *anyone* who wishes to communicate with spirits, as well as for the less adventurous who simply wish to satisfy their curiosity about the subject. Explore the nature of the Spiritual Body, learn how to prepare yourself to become a medium, experience for yourself the trance state, clairvoyance, psychometry, table tipping and levitation, talking boards, automatic writing, spiritual photography, spiritual healing, distant healing, channeling, development circles, and also learn how to avoid spiritual fraud.

0-87542-061-3, 272 pgs., 5 ¼x 8, illus., softcover $10.00

SECRETS OF GYPSY LOVE MAGICK
by Raymond Buckland, Ph.D.

One of the most compelling forms of magick—perhaps the most sought after—is love magick. It is a positive form of working, a way to true delight and pleasure. The Gypsies have long been known for the successful working of love magick.

In this book you will find magicks for those who are courting, who are newlyweds, and love magick for the family unit. There is also a section on Gypsy love potions, talismans and amulets.

Included are spells and charms to discover your future spouse, to make your lover your best friend and to bring love into a loveless marriage. You will learn traditional secrets gathered from English Gypsies that are presented here for the first time ever by a Gypsy of Romani blood.

0-87542-053-2, 176 pgs., mass market, illus. $3.95